Social-Cultural Anthropology

Social-Cultural Anthropology

Communication with the African Society

GEORGE ALLAN PHIRI

RESOURCE *Publications* • Eugene, Oregon

SOCIAL-CULTURAL ANTHROPOLOGY
Communication with the African Society

Resource Publications
A Division of Wipf and Stock Publishers
199 W. 8th Ave., Suite 3
Eugene, OR 97401
www.wipfandstock.com

ISBN 13: 978-1-60608-736-7

Manufactured in the U.S.A.

This work is dedicated to my beloved wife and companion in ministry, Hilda Phiri whose patience, observations and comments have invariably been significant.

Contents

List of Illustrations xi
Acronyms and Abbreviations xiii
Introduction xv

1 The Perspectives and Theories of Social-Cultural Anthropology 1
    Introduction
    Definitions: Anthropology, Culture and Worldview
    Elements of Culture: Theoretical Base of Social-Cultural
        Anthropology
    Cultural Influences
    Cultural Dynamics: Spiritual and Social Development
        Opportunities
    Culture and Worldview Formation

2 Anthropology, Social Development and Missions 19
    Introduction
    The Holistic View of the Community
    The Anthropological Worldview Concept
    The Anthropological Culture Concept
    Anthropological Culture Change
    Communication
    Anthropological Research Methods
    Data Collection and Analysis in Anthropological Study
    Discussion Questions

3 Incarnation and Interpersonal Relationships in Africa 31
    Introduction
    The Incarnation of Jesus Christ in the Jewish Culture
    The Incarnational Models for Cross-Cultural Workers
    Incarnation and Interpersonal Relationships
    Dicussion Questions

4   **Ethnographic Aspects of the African Society 41**
Introduction
The Society and the Social Structures
Definitions
Organization of the African Society
The Societal Impact on Church Growth
Discussion Questions

5   **Social Interactions and the Reality in Africa 54**
Introduction
Definition of Reality
Reality from Humanistic Perspective
Reality from God's Perspective
Social Interaction and Reality
Discussion Questions

6   **Communication and the African Social Structure 59**
Introduction
Definition of Cross-Cultural Communication
Social Relationships and Communication in Africa
The Effects of Social Structure on
        Cross-Cultural Communication in Africa
Discussion Questions

7   **Missiological Application of Social-Cultural Anthropology
        in Africa 66**
Introduction
The African Culture and Sin
Cultural Concept of Sin
Universal Concept of Sin
The Role of the Bible and the Holy Spirit on Sin
Discussion Questions

8   **The Missionary and African Culture Change 72**
Introduction
Reasons for Culture Change in Africa
The Role of a Missionary in Culture Change in Africa
Challenges to Culture Change in Africa
Facilitators of Culture Change in Africa
Managing the Results of Culture Change in Africa
Discussion Questions

9 The Church 81
        Introduction
        The Church as a Community
        The Church as an Institution
        Discussion Questions

10 Christian Leadership Development: An African Culture
            in Perspective 86
        Introduction
        African Cultural Leadership Models: Lessons
                for Post-Democratic Christian Leadership Aspirants
        Organization of the African Society
        Democratic African Leadership Model (DALM)
        Biblical Model of Electing Church Leadership
        Affirming the Role of the Holy Spirit in Developing
                Emerging Church Leaders
        Biblical Images of Leadership for the Church
                in African Cultural Context
        Basic Elements of Leadership in Africa
        The How of the African Leadership
        Importance of Christian Leadership in the Church
                and Society
        Typical Christian Leadership Images
        Evaluating the Call of African Christian Leaders into Ministry
        Conclusions
        Discussion Questions

11 Effective Pastoral Counseling Models for the African Community 122
        Introduction
        The Scope of this Study
        Definition of an African Marriage
        Universal African Traditions: The Framework
                for Pastoral Counseling in Africa
        The Evaluation of the Impact of Universal African Traditions
        African Risk Behavior and Vulnerability
                to HIV/AIDS pandemic
        The African Society and Counseling
                for Decision-Making Counseling
        Conclusions
        Discussion Questions

12 **Cohabitation Marriages: Biblical and Social Contemporary
        Perspectives 145**
    Introduction
    Background
    The Scope of this Chapter
    Definitions of Key Institutions
    Literature Review: The Challenges of Cohabitation
    The Challenges of Cohabitation
    The Roles of Institutions on Cohabitation
    Conclusions
    Discussion Questions

13 **Divorce: Spiritual and Socio-Economic Imact 164**
    Introduction
    The Analysis of African Marriage Relationships
    The Rationale of the Study
    The Spiritual Challenges of Divorce
    Divorce and Remarriage
    The Socio-Economic Challenges of Divorce
    Summary and Conclusions
    Discussion Questions

14 **The Humanitarian Ministry and Missions in Africa 175**
    Introduction
    The Theology of Humanitarian Ministry
    Biblical Model of Humanitarian Ministry
    Challenges of Christian Humanitarian Ministry
    Conclusions
    Discussion Questions

    Glossary 183
    Bibliography 185

List of Illustrations

Figure 1: Incarnational Model for Effective
                  Cross-Cultural Communication
Figure 2: A Traditional African Leadership Social Structure
Figure 3: Traditional African Administrative Structure.

Acronyms and Abbreviations

ADC	Area Development Committee
AIDS	Acquired Immunodefficiency Syndrome
DDC	District Development Committee
EAM	Evangelical Association of Malawi
GNB	Good News Bible
HIV	Human Immunodefficiency Virus
NKJV	New King James Version
STDs	Sexually Transmitted Diseases
STIs	Sexually Transmitted Infections
VDC	Village Development Committee
WLSA	Women and Law in Southern Africa

Introduction

UNDERSTANDING FACTORS THAT AFFECT effective communication with people of different cultural orientation is basic for successful ministry and social development work in any society. The challenges of Social development work, Missions and Church planting today, are more than ever before. They require studying people's thinking patterns, social structures and their integration with the culture of the society. History teaches that early missionaries did not take lessons on languages and social or cultural anthropology to study about cultures or worldviews of the respondent community in order to effectively facilitate communication of the gospel and social development work. Yet, it may be critically necessary to study these society's factors in order to facilitate communication of the gospel and social development services effectively.

The missionaries were just griped with the mission of God and they went everywhere without prior orientation to the peoples' cultures, social structures, thinking patterns, religions and languages. Some of these missionaries did not really go as missionaries but explorers and they identified the need of the gospel and other social amenities in the people they found at the spot when they interfaced with the people. And so, they ministered to them even without adequate preparation and knowledge of effective evangelistic methods of the gospel and orientation to the peoples' cultures, languages and worldviews. As a result, communication became the major challenge in their ministry. However, people's languages, cultures and value systems were in some places considered evil; resulting into Christianization of societies and misinterpretation of peoples' cultures and practices. Kenneth Scott Latourette records that Emperor Constantine in fear of losing political powers to Christians he Christianized the Roman Empire[1]. Christianization of Roman Empire had big impact on the spread of Christianity among the Roman territories during his time of reign. Nevertheless, this does

1. Latourette, *A History of Christianity*, 91–93.

not mean we should neglect the need for studying courses like Cultural or Social-Cultural Anthropology, Cross-Cultural communication, and Evangelism for missions and social work.

In reality, the early missionaries did not meet political, social and economic problems just as we do today. Almost all missionaries did not require a passport or a visa to enter into a country of their choice in the early centuries. But we learn from the same history that they had problems in communicating effectively with the indigenous people. Some problems that were prevalent were linguistic, culture, food and the recognition of the indigenous as people just as any other. These and other problems led some missionaries into attrition and a study of culture of people in some societies was critical.

Church planting, social and missions' work do not take place in a vacuum. They take place in an environment of diverse cultural, spiritual, economical, political and social integrations and challenges. Reality is therefore, considered relative because of diverse cultural, social, economic, political and religious worldviews. Scholars in different fields approach these issues differently depending on the emphasis of their studies.

The political worldviews, social structures, economic developments and religious systems the world has developed make missions and social work in some places more challenging today than ever before; yet in some places success is seen. These factors set the limits of social development, missions, church planting and church growth. For example, in the modern days, a missionary cannot be allowed to enter in any country without a passport. In other countries visa requirement is additional document the immigration office may ask from the person presenting a passport at the border post.

In some places, people of higher statuses usually do not associate with people of lower statuses. Social structures that have been developed in some societies today have actually grouped people in classes that make communication in some societies difficult between people of different classes; thus, creating a communication gap. For instance, the caste system is divided into higher and lower castes. Politics has categorized people into the elite and ordinary people usually called political cadres.

Further, the concepts of globalization and global village and culture need also to be defined in the context of missions, politics and social work. The study of Social-Cultural Anthropology is therefore significant for Social developers, Church planters and Missionaries of the twenty-first century in order to understand these concepts and apply them contextually. Missions is global in its perspective because it is an activity to be participated in by all believers from all nations to people of all nations in the whole world regardless of professional background, culture and economic status.

Social-Cultural Anthropology also lays a foundation for Cross-cultural communicators to identify inroads into any community or society for missions and social development work. Social-Cultural Anthropology covers theories and definitions of cultures, worldviews, social structures of the societies, religious beliefs and value systems and application of anthropological insights in communication to social development activities and missions on church planting and growth for both the church and the nation.

Since this is an introduction to Social-Cultural Anthropology, each chapter introduces and discusses anthropological theories and concepts for effective communication in the missionary work, and brings about an understanding of the society they occupy for social development work, missions and church planting. The chapters are divided further to develop the theories and concepts. At the end of each chapter there are questions to assess understanding before moving on to the next chapter. This will inherently help the reader to move with confidence and an understanding of the concepts to the next chapter.

The readers' understanding of the theories and concepts are evaluated through discussion questions at the end of each chapter. It is also advisable for the reader to approach the subject with sober mind. If the book is used as a text for the study of Social-Cultural Anthropology in a classroom situation, the most plausible approach is that a lecturer should resume a responsibility of a facilitator rather than of a lecturer so that students' participation in the lessons is potentially maximized and appreciate their contribution in the lesson. Peter Ngatia and Alfred Mutema observes that "the current trend in teaching and learning is to promote active interaction between teachers and students so that students take responsibility for their own learning"[2]

---

2. Ngatia and Mutema, *Principles and Practices of Problem-Based Learning,* 4.

1

The Perspectives and Theories
of Social-Cultural Anthropology

- Introduction
- Definitions: Anthropology, Culture and Worldview
- Elements of Culture: Theoretical Base of Social-Cultural Anthropology
- Cultural Influences
- Cultural Dynamics
- Culture and Worldview
- Discussion Questions

INTRODUCTION

THE OBJECTIVE OF THIS chapter is to introduce readers to anthropological theories, terminologies, reasons for studying Social-Cultural Anthropology and the concept of Incarnation as research approach in ministry and social work. It is also important to realize that the terms defined in this chapter do not provide the exhaustive list of terminologies in Social-Cultural Anthropology and other anthropological studies. However, what this chapter provides is the starter pack to the reader to develop the anthropological concepts and vocabulary. It is based on the assumption that the reader is taking this course of study for the first time. Therefore, it is imperative for the reader to grasp the meaning of the concepts quickly and conceptualize them in one's own vocabulary. For this reason, the concepts are defined succinctly.

Further, this chapter introduces the reader to missiological and sociological concepts of anthropology and its relationship to social development, missions and church planting. Therefore, the reader is urged to understand the concepts and know how to apply them in his/her daily ministry and social work cross-culturally.

DEFINITIONS: ANTHROPOLOGY, CULTURE AND WORLDVIEW

Anthropology

Anthropology is one of the social and human behavioral sciences. The word anthropology comes from two Greek words *anthrop* and *logos*. *Anthrop* simply means man and *logos* mean study of. Hence, anthropology means the study of man; how he thinks, communicates, and behaves in his social-cultural environment.

In Social-Cultural Anthropology, the interest is in the study of the society's thinking patterns, communication loop, and man's behavior in his cultural setting and how culture affects the preaching of the gospel and communication in social development of the community. Charles Kraft says, "You cannot put people into the test tubes or into books."[1] It is very true that people are not studied in a laboratory setting in anthropology. Social-Cultural Anthropology as a discipline of study studies people through participatory action research by observing their behaviors, rituals, beliefs, value systems, and attitudes in their cultural setting. It also studies people through incarnation in their daily religious, cultural, and social rituals and work. The behaviors and attitudes are influenced by the assumptions of reality conceptualized in the worldview of the society or an individual's cultural principles of life.

Social-Cultural Anthropologists just as any other social scientists conduct research. In most cases, social-cultural anthropological research is qualitative rather than quantitative. However, it is important to recognized that social anthropologists also conduct quantitative research and their findings are reported as it is the case in any social science academic pursuit. Now if a man cannot be put in the test tube or in books, how can social anthropologist study man objectively? Usually, the social-cultural anthropological research because of its nature it is subjective; yet reliable. This is because it is done in practice setting. Anthropologists study people through incarnation in the respondent society, through

1. Charles Kraft, *Anthropology for Christian Witness*, 12.

personal participation and observing the changes in behaviors, rituals, beliefs, values, and attitudes of people in the society where they live and how the beliefs, rituals and values help develop and affect the behaviors of people in the society toward human and social development. Social-Cultural Anthropology studies are both quantitative and qualitative in nature. Hence, it is important to realize that their conclusions are as objective, subjective and reliable as any other social science studies.

People everywhere think and behave according to how they perceive things to be like and defined in the context of their cultural, social, economic and religious orientation. Therefore, studying them anthropologically enhances the understanding of their spiritual, political and social behavior and needs.

Culture

The English word culture embraces several meanings depending on who defines it. Politicians, economists, anthropologists, theologians and sociologists define culture in the context of the emphasis of their studies. Hence, the meaning of the word culture is subjective. Clyde Kluckholn defines culture as a way of thinking, feeling, and believing. It is the group's knowledge stored up for future use."[2] Louis Luzbetak defines culture as a set of norms, standards, notions, and beliefs.[3] Paul Hiebert says that culture is more or less integrated systems of ideas, feelings, and values and their associated patterns of behavior and products shared by a group of people who organize and regulate what they think, feel and do.[4] There is one thing that is common to all of the preceding definitions. Culture is the expression of the society's reality and attitudes through feelings, beliefs, values and behavioral patterns.

Culture may also be defined as integrated belief and value systems of a society and how that society perceives and interprets reality, behaviors, and communication symbols and articulate their philosophy of life in a practical way. Culture serves as an identity of a society. It also sets the value and belief systems of a society in order of their perception of reality. People can easily be known by their culture and language rather than their skin color and other identities. However, it is imperative to realize

2. Kluckholn, *Mirror for Man*, 23.

3. Luzbetak, *The Church and Cultures*, 156.

4. Hiebert, *Anthropological Insights for Missionaries*, 30.

that culture is not the only identity of people in any society. There are also other unique features that identify the society; such as, clothes, food, and eating habits and so forth. These are critical factors in describing the society's cultural identity.

Worldview

Worldview is the framework of human-centered assumptions about good and evil, right or wrong as perceived by the reality of an individual or a society. Reality is assumed in the worldview of the individual and the society.

Larry Niemeyer observes that worldview is the basis of religion.[5] In fact, worldview is how a person or a society perceives the world and assumes its reality; religiously or secularly and interpret it in practical way that determines the universal behavior of the society or an individual. In most cases reality defines the Supreme Being revered in that particular religion and a society. The Supreme Being revered in the society always has an influence on the perception of things and an interpretation of events and issues in the society. Worldview influences the thinking patterns of the adherents of a particular culture and how they perceive themselves and others in a real and imaginary world. King David said that he was a worm (Psalm 22:6). This was his perception about himself in relation to God and other people who surrounded him. Nevertheless, this perception does not imply that he lost his self-esteem. It was an expression of humility before God, his creator and the world around him.

Worldview is learnt consciously and or unconsciously. No one actually questions why s/he perceives things the way s/he does; until such a time when that reality is challenged due to illumination of the mind about the view or exposure to new information, knowledge and experiences that make sense more than the long time held view. Certainly, this affects how and what people think and believe in as true or false, good or evil. James W. Sire defines worldview as a set of presuppositions which we hold (consciously or unconsciously) about the basic make-up of our world.[6] Marguerite Kraft defines worldview as the basic assumptions, values, and allegiances of a group of people.[7]

5. Niemeyer, *Cultural Anthropology: Cultural Studies for Ministry Practitioners*, 5.

6. Sire, *Scripture Twisting*, 25.

7. Marguerite Kraft, *Understanding Spiritual Power: A Forgotten Dimension of Cross-Cultural*

Any social development worker, missionary or church planter who overlooks the respondent society's worldview may be in danger of misinterpreting and misunderstanding the society and then, fail to communicate the gospel and successfully implement social development work in more effective way. Basically, worldview forms the belief and value systems of the society and it bases its decisions on how the reality is understood in the context of their culture. Eventually, the society's actions are motivated and directed by their perception of reality of their world and then, behave in certain ways. Worldview also influences the adherents of a particular view to think in certain way; and then, behave accordingly.

ELEMENTS OF CULTURE: THEORETICAL BASE OF SOCIAL-CULTURAL ANTHROPOLOGY

1. LANGUAGE

This is a basic cultural element of anthropology in communication. Every society has a language for communication. Language is part of the people's culture, belief and value systems of the society because it expresses *what* and *how* people communicate with each other within or outside the society. The words used in any language express what and how people in a particular society perceive and interpret the reality. A word has no meaning on its own unless it represents the actual thing in a real life situation. Missionaries and social development workers learn the people's languages in order to communicate the gospel and social development knowledge, information and concepts effectively in the peoples' own languages to enhance understanding. Effective communication with the respondent society is basic to the success of any project; be it religious, social or economic.

In any society, people communicate in audible or silent language. Edward Hall observes that silent language of the culture is mysterious to missionaries.[8] Usually, communication breakdown between the missionaries, social development experts, and the respondent society occurs because of the mystery of silent language. Silent language is either taken for granted or misunderstood and misinterpreted by missionaries and social development experts in a foreign culture. As a result, the

Mission and Ministry, 21.

8. Hall, *The Silent Language.* Silent language is the most obscure communication symbol in any society.

intended projects fail to realize the goals anticipated at the beginning of the project. Being able to greet someone in their own language will help you enjoy your contact with local people even more while visiting Africa and the effort will certainly be appreciated.[9]

Communication in every society is either verbal or nonverbal; sometimes both are used. Effective communication of the gospel and social interventions in any society needs to consider audible, sign and silent languages in which the respondent community communicates. Silent language can only be learnt effectively if there is personal interaction with the respondent society through incarnation and participation in societal activities. Precisely, this helps the communicator to understand what the people say, do and how they express themselves through body language in their society and then, respond accordingly. Language also shows how people express their emotions. Certain words, when they are used can tell whether the person is emotionally happy or not. For example, in English, words like, stupid! Foolish! May express emotional annoyance or anger! It is necessary therefore, to learn and understand both audible and silent language of the respondent society for effective gospel and social development communication.

In Africa, oftentimes people communicate orally through storytelling. Basically, oral communication in Africa may yield tremendous results for gospel and social development work. It is therefore important to learn peoples' language and systems of communication in Africa for effective communication.

2. FOOD

Different people have different food tastes and appreciate food differently. Anthropologically, food expresses the society's worldview of their reality about what is edible, tasty and what is not. Generally, people learn eating different foods at home unconsciously except in certain circumstances where one encounters new food stuffs in a foreign cultural setting. For example, Africans have diverse food recipes; ranging from fried flying ants, larva to biltong.[10] Often members of the society assume that all people everywhere have the same food tastes and preferences. In Africa, when a visitor visits your home you prepare food for him or her without

9. Africa Travel, "*People and Culture of Africa*" para. 35.

10. Africa Travel, "Food and Drinks", para. 13.

asking whether that visitor eats the food you have prepared or not. The assumption is that for the visitor to feel welcomed must be provided with food and that s/he eats the same food tastes like yours. Africans eat certain foods that may exasperate or surprise a visitor from the Western society. For example, certain types of caterpillars and mice are edible in Africa by most traditional Africans. This is a challenge to Western missionaries and social workers in Africa; especially those who come to Africa with food biases. This situation creates cultural food shocks in the missionaries and social workers. Traditionally, if you refuse to eat the food that was prepared for you in Africa, you are either considered to be proud or you do not accept or respect the person who offered you that food. The result of this may be rejection of you and your message in the respondent society.

Food is considered as one of the most important element of any culture, particularly in Africa. Therefore, Western missionaries and social workers should prepare to incarnate in the food recipes of Africans; although adjustment is not as easy. Rejection of the respondent society's food recipes mainly in Africa may result in rejection of the gospel or hinder effective communication with the respondent society. Hence, missionaries and social workers to Africa need to understand why some missionaries have yielded insignificant missions results or failed in Africa. On the other hand, it must be understood that traditional Africans cannot prepare the food that would comparatively appeal to the western missionary's food recipes. Food is only good and tasty to the people who eat it unconsciously. It does not matter how nutritious it may be. Some Africans are psychologically allergic to some western foods just as the westerners are to African food favorites. Thus, missionaries and extension social development workers may incarnate in food recipes to develop effective relationship with the respondent African society for effective communication.

3. Dressing Mode.

People dress according to how they perceive their world economically, geographically, socially and religiously. The scriptures that talk about dressing for example (Deut 22:5)[11] need clear and contextual interpreta-

---

11. There is history and culture related to what God was addressing in the Jewish society of Moses' generation in Deutronomy 22:5. One must first, understand how clothes were made distinct to their gender and the reason for putting up a cloth of a different gender; otherwise, interpretation may be heretic.

tion in the cross-cultural society; otherwise, the missionary can experience difficulties in communicating the gospel in a new culture in Africa and anywhere in the world. In fact, the missionary and every social worker need to consider geographical, economic, social and religious factors that affect, and influence the society to favor certain patterns of dressing. Some factors that determine what type of dressing people put on are the occasions and weather changes. For example, climatic changes may compel people to change their mode of dressing to defeat the weather conditions. Sometimes the occasion like wedding or funeral and other cultural celebrations may compel people to put on a dress that may express the significance of the occasion in their culture. Further, the social class to which the person belongs in the society and the wealth a person owns, also economically influences his/her dressing mode.

Religion and the economic status of the society also have greater influence on the dressing mode of the people in Africa as well as anywhere else in the world. Certain religions require their adherents to be putting on certain type of dressing to signify their faith, allegiance and positions in that religion.

The society in a Christian or Muslim dominated areas may adopt Christian or Islamic way of dressing; although there is no Christian dressing. What is considered as modest dressing by the society may depend also on how their culture, economy and religion define modest and social-moral standards. Therefore, a cross-cultural communicator should consider poverty, modest and nakedness as subjective and objective only to the adherents of the particular culture and society's norms.

An African may be putting on a ragged short and walk bare footed. A person from western cultural orientation may consider such a person poor. In some cases this is true; yet in other cases this scenario is deceptive. They require contextual description. For example, the traditional *Swazi* dressing in Swaziland would tantamount to nakedness in the cultural context of some Africans and some Westerners; yet in the *Swazis'* perception it is modest dressing; as one *Swazi* confided in me. Further, the attitudes of the society on the description of modest and immodest is conceptualized in the worldview of what is acceptable by the society's reality and morality. Critical understanding of this is particularly important to avoid prejudices and misinterpretations on the part of the cross-cultural communicator.

4. Thinking Patterns

People's behavior and actions are determined by peoples' thinking about themselves and others. Every culture impacts and influences its adherents' thinking patterns through its beliefs in Supreme Being (religion), rituals and values (social-cultural) and interpretation of reality in a particular society. As such, it is imperative for the missionary and the social worker to study the respondent cultures' economy and religion carefully in order to effectively communicate the gospel and implement social development projects in any society. "For as he thinks in his heart so is he" (Prov.23:7 [NKJV]).

Psychologically, peoples' thinking patterns about what is right or wrong, righteous or evil, tasty or tasteless, modest or immodest depends on *what* and *how* their religious, economic, political and social worldviews define those concepts. For that reason, society's thinking patterns are subjective because they are largely influenced by their religion and socio-cultural concepts that are believed differently in different societies. The way the people think about themselves and toward others, influences how they behave and perform their cultural rituals and economic activities in their society.

5. Relationship Patterns

Culture is a determinant factor of how people of opposite gender or the same gender, of the same or different age levels relate with each other in the society, publicly or privately. In some societies, people observe gender and age distinctions in public worship services and work places; although, this trend diminishes with current social and religious developments in the human rights, freedoms and cultural syncretism. But in some African societies, gender and age distinctions are still observed in many ways; especially in public religious and social gatherings. In Malawi and Zambia, for example; women, children and men do not just mix in their seating plan in the church. Usually, women sit on one side of the church and men on the other; but in the same auditorium. They sit opposite each other. However, in very few churches men and women sit randomly besides each other; especially married women sitting next to their husbands. Such churches are considered 'English' churches (multinational and multi-lingual churches).

There are also culturally defined jobs specifically for women and men in some African societies. For example, cooking, nursing and home making are culturally considered as the work for women in Malawi and some African countries; while hunting, grave digging as work for men; although this trend is experiencing paradigm shift in modern Africa. Thus, the missionary in his/her endeavor to communicate the gospel and do social work in Africa need to understand how people relate and observe gender distinctions in the African society. This trend and thinking pattern is drastically changing in the modern African societies. There are also male nurses in Malawi; for example.

In Africa, boys and girls when they are at adolescence stage of their development they are separated in the home and taught different survival skills and roles according to their gender and age. They are made aware of their gender differences and other moral and ethical issues following their age and gender. The separation of boys and girls according to their gender and age has relationship impact on the thinking patterns of the boys and girls in the African society.

It is this gender sensitivity at early age that may develop into gender discrimination and inequalities later in life. Most traditional African parents still believe that there is natural inequality between boys and girls, men and women; that they have different strength and perception of things; therefore, they should be taught different survival skills and roles. They are also encouraged at this age to sleep in different bedrooms and take bath separately in the same home.

At the age of adolescence, young people are exposed to gender and age differences and relationships; and they make a lot of gender decisions separately. Gender based violence; inequalities and discrimination are serious issues in Africa today. The Ministry of gender and child welfare in Malawi has developed policies to reduce gender inequalities and disparities.[12] They are probably influenced by cultural communication systems and perception of the society about gender early in life or gender-related violence.

Some churches in Africa do not recognize women leadership in the church. The reasons being gender misconceptions, misinformation and failure to recognize God's calling of women into ministry and the purpose of the Holy Spirit baptism for missions to the ends of the earth that

12. Ministry of gender and child welfare, *Gender Policy in Malawi.*

included women (Acts 1:8, 14–15). God has called people of both genders into ministry of his word. He has empowered people of both genders with the Holy Spirit and skills for communicating the gospel and social development to people of all nations. Therefore, it is important to understand the role played by the society in gender realization, actualization and practice in social and human development of any nation.

CULTURAL INFLUENCES

1. Marriages

In Africa, people practice monogamy, polygamy, cohabitation and endogamous marriages. Homosexual marriages are not common in Africa; yet they exist. Those who practice homosexual marriages claim that it is their human and constitutional right in the countries where homosexuality has been constitutionalized. For example, South African government has legalized gay marriages. In most African societies, homosexuality is considered evil, morally and ethically unacceptable marriage; in most cases, those who practice homosexual marriages are discriminated against. These types of marriages are a result of cultural and religious influences. However, it is also important to recognize that religion and economy also have impact on whether a person should have multiple wives or not; to practice heterosexual, homosexual and cohabitation marriages or not.

It is a common belief in Africa that there should be children in every marriage. The absence of children in many marriages has led to the breakdown or divorce in those marriages in Africa.[13] This is probably one reason why homosexual marriages are not common in Africa; because children are expected in every marriage. Therefore, apart from observing religious influence on the rejection of homosexual marriages in Africa, culture also has an impact on the rejection of homosexual marriages in the African society.

Incest is prohibited in most African societies. In some traditional African societies girls at puberty stage are given in sexual affair with someone for sexual maturity approval for girls as it was the case among the *Luvale* tribe in Zambia. In those communities, a girl was allowed to have sex with someone with permission from elderly women to approve

13. Malunda and Mpinganjira, *Social and Development Studies Book* 3, 130–34, and Chondoka, *Traditional Marriages in Zambia: A Study in Cultural History,* 13.

her maturity and readiness for marriage after she has gone through the puberty stage.[14] However, it is imperative to understand that no one marries a virgin in the societies where someone else does have sex with girls after puberty. Even in this cultural practice, incest is prohibited. In modern Africa, those who practice incest are condemned by the society because the practice has healthy risks and considered unchristian, immoral and unethical. This practice was common among the *Luvale* tribes in Northern Zambia. The practice has since changed because of the influence of Christianity and the fear to contract Sexual Transmitted Diseases (STDs), Sexual Transmitted Infections (STIs) and HIV/AIDS.

2. SOCIAL STRUCTURES

In every culture people have statuses and roles. The statuses define the classes and positions of people in the society. The status and a role a person holds and plays in a society or church is largely influenced by culturally approved and described positions and the perception of leadership in the society.

Leadership in any society develops as a result of social structure; social, economic and spiritual needs in that particular society and the external influence of the same. The status fosters and vests certain responsibility, authority and power on people holding certain positions in the society. In Africa, if a person is a potential emerging leader and he/she does not belong to a royal family s/he may not be considered for a higher status of leadership in that kingdom. Potential emerging leaders in the kingdom may not be developed into society's leaders just because they do not belong to the royal family. Nevertheless, civil leaders are developed from mere ordinary society members who demonstrate unique leadership qualities. Political leaders for example are not developed from royal families. Therefore, it is important for the church to recruit and develop potential emerging Christian leaders from the people who are spirit-filled, mature, and wise and have good reputation in the church and the society (Acts 6:3). The church must provide a parallel model of leadership to that of the royal lineage in the African society.

14. Ibid, 13–14.

3. GENDER AND WORK

In some societies work is divided according to gender. Oftentimes, in Africa men consider women to be vulnerable to certain jobs and positions. As a result, work has been classified according to gender. In many African countries women are not accepted as duly bona fide ministers of the gospel. In Botswana for example, people deserted the church because their denomination ordained a woman to be a pastor of a certain local congregation.[15] As a result, there are a few women ministers of the gospel in Africa. And where they are accepted, women have difficulties to make it into church leadership.[16] Nevertheless, gender discrimination, inequalities and biases are losing ground in the modern African societies. Most African societies are realizing the importance of respecting people of opposite gender for various jobs, professions and positions of leadership in the church and the society. The study by Mufune and Mwansa states that Malawi and Zimbabwe have been very successful in agricultural programs simply because of integrating women in averting hunger and household economic difficulty.[17] Recognition of women in Africa is also experienced in the political development. Some women have been elected and appointed to high offices; for example, the president of Liberia, Ellen Johnson Sirleaf, Africa's first woman president. On December 8, 2004 Joyce Mujuru was sworn in as the Zimbabwe's vice president just to mention but a few. This is a dawn of actualizing recognition of women in positions of political leadership in Africa. It is also hoped that this trend will extend its impact in religious institutions.

Women population everywhere in the world is at more than one half of the population.[18] Yet they are the most neglected and vulnerable socially to social and spiritual empowerment. Gender disparity is widening also because of feminism theories. There is a need to look at the difference between the theories of gender and feminism critically in order to deal with issues of inequalities in gender and work.

15. Botswana Television *News,* April 2008.

16. Phiri, "Women Empowerment for Missions: A Capacity Building Program for a Local Church," *Master of Arts Capstone Project,* 43.

17. Mufune and Mwansa, "Supervisory Women and Men in Work Organizations", 38.

18. Megyery, *Women in Canadian Politics: Toward Equity in Representation,* 3.

4. Age

Universally, a person who is below 18 years of age is described in the UN charter as a child; therefore, s/he cannot marry unless with parental or guardian consent. First, the concept of parental or guardian consent implies cultural influence on the decision. This means that the definition of age has cultural impact as well. Second, in Africa, age is culturally considered as an element of experience and wisdom to those who are old and the young generation. This is why counseling in African societies is considered to be the work of elderly people; and leadership appointments also consider age.

The church is one of the institutions involved in wedding people in Africa. The government and the society recognize wedding the couples as the function of the church. Therefore, it is important for the missionary or pastors to understand the impact of age to the respondent African society. The church must collaborate with other stakeholders on the definition of age to avoid wedding children into marriage.

5. Interpersonal Relationships

How people communicate and relate to each other is highly determined by the society's religion, perception of gender and social structure. For example, in Muslim societies women and men have separate worship places. Laurie Goodstein observes that women have pushed to remove partitions or walls or simply the rules that prevent women worshipers from seeing or hearing the imam.[19] Although Muslim women seek to sit in the same chamber or auditorium with men for worship, most African women and men spend much of their time separately. They usually meet at night when going to bed in case of those who are married. Gender and divisions of work in African society expedite this. Men and women do different jobs in different places according to how division of labour is understood in African context. In Africa, interpersonal relationship also considers and faces gender challenges and discrimination.

Missionaries and social development workers need to be people-oriented. They need to be adaptable to the respondent society as George Fotis states that adaptability is still a major positive force in our continuing survival, but in a totally different context.[20] Consequently, this may

---

19. Goodstein, "Muslim Women Seeking a Place in the Mosque," para 4.
20. Fotis, "9 Most Powerful Ways to Improve Your People Skills", 35–45.

help the missionary or the social worker understand the people and their problems better. Interpersonal relationship is vital for gospel communication and the success of the social and human development interventions in any society because people are considered as a community and ministered to holistically. In addition, interpersonal relationships enhance peoples' participation in the spiritual and social development activities.

In Africa, people view themselves as a community. They belong to one another. They consider face to face communication, personal presence and sharing their belongings as the most valuable elements of their African culture. Most Africans, because of their oral and community orientation have developed interpersonal communication skills for easy communication and interaction. It is imperative to realize that African society is dependent on interpersonal relationships. Certainly, this enhances effective communication in the African society.

CULTURAL DYNAMICS: SPIRITUAL AND SOCIAL DEVELOPEMNT OPPORTUNITIES

Culture is dynamic. There is no culture in the world that is static and survives by itself without the influence of another. Every culture is in the process of transition from long time held views to something that is challenging and makes sense in the contemporary world. It is influenced by political, technological, religious, educational, social, healthy and economic development or something else that makes sense in another culture or community. The assumption is that the newly discovered knowledge is likely to work better if adopted into the existing culture and pool of knowledge than what the society might have held for a long time as the best. This is the major factor affecting cultural changes in the present world of dynamics.

Global culture seems economically, politically and spiritually challenging and good to embrace. Peter Lwaminda declares that cultural imperialism in Africa is driven by new technologies and profit propensities of the dynamics of globalization.[21] So, many things and practices in every culture are changing. Adaptation of new ideas into the existing belief and value systems of any culture or organization eventually results in culture change and enhances spiritual, human and social development

21. Lwaminda, "The Church as Family and the Quest for Justice and Peace in Africa", 261.

of the society. The cultural changes that are taking place in every society are the opportunities for socio-economic development of the society and to the reaching out to the nations with the gospel of Jesus Christ. The church planters and missionaries should be on the lookout and take advantage of the cultural changes for the gospel and social development. It is also imperative to realize that the holistic gospel approach in respect of people's cultures certainly makes sense to the society and eventually people may opt for it rather than the long time held views that may not make sense in the present challenging social, spiritual and economic life of the society.

In the twenty-first century, cultural changes are mainly influenced by political, economical, religious, educational and sociological developments taking place in the world. Missions is done in such culturally dynamic environments. Missiologists and social workers must change their strategies for missions and social work respectively with times and events. "You must change with times unless you are big enough to change the times"[22] (Anonymous).

Every culture is modifying itself by incorporating syncretically or adapting in what others have discovered to be working for the good of individuals or the entire society. This modification is constantly breaking long time held views about what a particular society held to be true, good or effective.

Every person in the society wants to be successful either in the world of education, business, politics or religion. Richard Bellingham says, "We have found there are three key success factors in changing corporate culture efforts... developing capacity accelerates the process, and aligning the culture sustains whatever changes are achieved."[23] Social workers, Church planters and missionaries need to appreciate cultural dynamism; and then, strategize for missions. Cultural changes are not for their own sake; but to create opportunities for missions and socio-economic development of the society too.

Africans have always been described as idol worshipers and that their religion is syncretism and animistic. In some cases this is true; yet in another it is not. Due to cultural dynamics, Africans are among the true and spiritual worshipers. It is wrong to generalize the worship of Africans as if

22. Luzbetak, *The Church and Cultures: New Perspectives in Missiological Anthropology*, 292.

23. Bellingham, *Corporate Culture Change*, 9.

all Africans are animistic or idol worshipers. There are remnant true worshipers of God in Africa. Christian Mhagama states that Pope John Paul II appealed to theologians in Africa to develop the theology of the church as a family; demonstrating its complementarity with other images of the church in the world.[24] Therefore, Africans should not only be perceived as animistic and idol worshipers; but as true worshipers of a true God also. Although it is observed that some Africans are syncretic and idolatry in their religion, it is not right to generalize African worship too much.

The gospel is another factor for culture change. Some long time held religious, social, political and economic views in many cultures in Africa are detrimental to the gospel communication and social and human development; especially in Africa. Hence, the preaching of the gospel has changed those views and people have been liberated from views that would have delayed even socio-economic and political development of their society. Church planters, missionaries and those engaged in social development work of the African society should be aware of such changes. The gospel initiatives should strive to bring about change of such views through demonstration of Christ—centered love, humility of servant-hood leadership and biblical teachings in the society. However, critical study of the particular culture is essential before any changes are implemented because not all in African culture is lost and evil as some may suppose. As a matter of fact, social workers, missionaries and church planters need to strategize changes toward the goal of their mission in a particular African society.

CULTURE AND WORLDVIEW FORMATION

"Culture is the label anthropologists give to the structured customs and underlying worldview assumptions which govern peoples' lives."[25] Culture is the observable phenomenon in every society. It is the product of worldview which influences what and how people think, behave and align their everyday lives and interpretation of reality. People perceive and define reality in terms of their worldview and then, determine how they should behave, live and respond to situations that affect them and other people in their society.

24. Mhagama, "Pauline Churches as God's Family a Search from the Roots," 183–84.
25. Charles Kraft, "Culture, Worldview and Contextualization", 385.

When the gospel comes, they perceive it from what their reality (worldview) tells them to be true. Kraft also notes that peoples' worldview determines their view of reality.[26] The effect of the understanding of their reality is the action they take toward communication and culture change in their society.

Therefore, if a social worker, church planter or a missionary wants to bring a social or spiritual change in the society what needs to be changed is the worldview of the respondent society not necessarily the culture. Culture changes automatically when new and appealing concepts have been adopted into the existing culture. It is only when the reality is perceived as reality in the context of the gospel and the social work in the society; the change may not be significant and necessary. Charles Kraft treats culture and worldview as one thing that is inclusive. Then, change needs to target both.

Social subsystems in Cultural Anthropology explain the shapes of society's worldview, thinking patterns and people's behavioral expressions that are influenced by those subsystems. Thus, the gospel and social development efforts need to be directed toward these subsystems and thereby transform the humanistic, idolatry, and lazy worldviews and the society's mindset. When people are truly challenged socially, mentally and spiritually, they begin demonstrating transformed attitudes and behavior in all their cultural life. The indigenous church that really reflects converted life will have to align its cultural beliefs with changed attitudes, values, beliefs, and behavior as a result of Christ's spirit indwelling them.

DISCUSSION QUESTIONS:

- How does Anthropology differ from other Social Sciences?
- Define Culture in relation to worldview.
- Why should the gospel target to change the people's worldview rather than their culture?

26. Ibid., 385.

2

Anthropology, Social Development and Missions

- Introduction
- The Holistic View of the Community
- The Anthropological Worldview Concept
- The Anthropological Culture Concept
- Anthropological Culture Change
- Communication
- Anthropological Research Methods
- Data Collection and Analysis in Anthropological Study
- Discussion Questions

INTRODUCTION

SOCIAL DEVELOPMENT AND MISSIONS benefit a lot from studying anthropology as an academic pursuit. Social development and Missions are about people; not things. To better understand people why they do what they do, why they eat what they eat is to study them as a whole in their cultural setting not in laboratory and in segments. Anthropology studies people holistically and provides means of understanding people's behavior, their culture, and worldview, how they think and respond to views different from theirs. This is foundational to developing communication channels for missions and social development work.

Missiology and Social Sciences study how God through Christ, the Church and individual Christians can effectively communicate the gospel and social interventions and become a blessing to people of all nations. He promised Abraham ". . . all peoples on earth will be blessed through you" (Gen 12:3). The gospel is God's expression of love through Jesus Christ;

the Son of David, the Son of Abraham (Matt 1:1) to bless all nations on earth. The apostle Paul commenting on the same said, "How beautiful are the feet of those who bring good news!" (Rom 10:15).

In this chapter, we will study how a social worker, a missionary or a church planter can become a blessing to the people being reached with the gospel. Missiology and Anthropology as a social science complement each other in fulfilling the task of social and community development, church planting and missions.

THE HOLISTIC VIEW OF THE COMMUNITY

A community or a society is not a disjointed institution. A community is a spiritual, political, social and economic institution. A missionary or a social worker needs to understand the spiritual, political, social and economic structures and relationships of a community. Members of a society are connected together in one way or another. Culture is one of the elements that bonds people together in the society. It is this connectivity that missionaries and the social, and community development workers need to critically study and understand in order to share the gospel and any social work more effectively. The relationships that exist in any society have moral and ethical effect on how people of a particular society think, communicate, behave and work. The community and individual's activities in any society are influenced by what their worldview has taught them. Culture is a product of learning and adaptation. The young generation learns from the older generation about beliefs, values and communication networks unconsciously. "Anthropologists are not only interested in how people think but also in what people do in their everyday activities."[1] You cannot claim that you know a man by studying only how he thinks. In fact, there are various factors that influence thinking in an individual or the society. Spiritual, psychological, social and economic problems in the community influence the thinking processes of individuals and eventually the entire society. Hence, studying what people eat, dress, work, believe, and how they express joy, grief, anger, worship and so forth is significant.

Anthropologists are interested in the whole man. Whatever man thinks, and does depends on how s/he perceives the reality and influence the behavior of that person or the society. The perception of reality is de-

1. Charles Kraft, *Anthropology for Christian Witness*, 4.

veloped from the conceived worldview of the society whether consciously or unconsciously. Therefore, Social-Cultural Anthropology can be of great help to social and community development workers, missionaries and church planters by providing them with knowledge about the factors which influence the thinking processes, responses and the belief and value systems of their societies.

Culture is a total sum of conceptualized values, beliefs and rituals that are in constant practice in the society by adherents of that culture. How people think, behave and do what they do is largely regulated by their cultural worldview and understanding of reality. Therefore, church planters, missionaries and social and community development workers need to play a critical role to learn and understand the people's culture before ministering the gospel to them or launching any development program. As much as you have your biases as a missionary from another cultural orientation, the respondent society also has its biases toward foreigners. To trade biases of the missionary with that of the respondent society has always been a challenge to most missionaries and social development workers; particularly in Africa. Yet it is the best way to find a premise for the gospel communication and community development work cross-culturally. Careful study of anthropology creates several inroads into the respondent culture that can eventually enhance the preaching of the gospel and social, and community development activities in any society.

Social-Cultural Anthropology looks at the whole society; its make-up, language, food, dressing mode, communication networks, symbols, etc in order to understand the society before it assumes how to approach the people with the gospel and social and community development interventions. People must be treated holistically not as souls without body and spirit or as economic casualties. People are human beings with a soul, body and spirit. This is a crucial concept for effective church planting, missionary work and social, and community development in any society. The community needs spiritual, social and economic solutions to their problems. It does not matter who addresses the problems; whether the church or any concerned institution, the problems must be solved. People are body, soul and spirit and they must be treated as such.

THE ANTHROPOLOGICAL WORLDVIEW CONCEPT

Culture is based on the society's worldview. And the Worldview is formed from the basic assumptions of beliefs, value systems, and allegiances that members of the particular society give to that culture and reality.

In many African societies, there is a belief in spirits. For example, in some African societies when a person is eating food, and suddenly a chunk of food falls out of hand it is believed that the spirit has taken it and that person does not bother to get it back. Another example in African context is what the West calls elderly mentality; in Africa, elders are always right, experienced and wise. Hence, command obedience and allegiance from younger generation. Things like these interpret the worldview of the African society and the adherents of its culture. The behavior of people is therefore influenced by their interpretation of reality which includes their worldview of the spirit world and the age respectively.

The value people give to their culture in every society determines whether personal decision for Christ should be expected in public or not. Usually I tend to speculate that Nicodemus in John chapter 3 belonged to a society that had respect and allegiance to communal relationships and decision-making. So, he could not talk to Jesus Christ on personal level in public. That is why he made it at night with Jesus to avoid embarrassment and rejection from the society.

In every culture people behave according to what they have learnt and conceptualized in their worldview as reality. The interpretation of reality in any culture depends on their worldview. Therefore, when ministering in certain African societies particularly those dominated by Islamic religion, the issue of raising hands in public to indicate personal decision for Christ may not be appropriate. Sometimes this is also influenced by communalism of the African society. Decision making in Africa, as it is also said elsewhere in this book, is a consultative process.

THE ANTHROPOLOGICAL CULTURE CONCEPT

Charles Kraft says, "But there is something in between the physical and the environmental, something intangible but very real and very influential in human life. This is the thing we call 'culture.'"[2] Culture is neither physical nor biological but environmental. Culture is influential on how people think, behave, work and live; and what they do in

2. Charles Kraft, *Anthropology for Christian Witness*, 6.

their everyday life. Is it biologically inherited or how does it influence people's mind so powerfully?

Culture is not biologically inherited. It is learnt, adapted, adopted, and syncretically integrated into the existing beliefs, rituals and value systems of the society. In the previous discussion, I stated that culture is dynamic; and that no culture is static or immune of external influence for change. Anthropologically, no culture is without features learnt and adopted from another influential culture or technological development. For example, language is full of borrowed words from other languages; such as, the English word, evangelism comes from Greek word *evangelion.*[3]

We develop culture consciously and or unconsciously. No person is born with a culture. Culture is learnt as the older generation formats the present and future generations in thought processes to consider what they considered to be right or wrong, good or evil, danger or safe, acceptable or unacceptable, tasty or tasteless, etc to become part of us. Later in life, we add to or deduct from previously conceptualized views that make or does not make sense in our present day from what the environment offers. Interaction with people from other cultural orientation also brings some beliefs, values, thinking patterns that challenge long time held views about right or wrong, good or bad, acceptable or unacceptable etc. We are then left with a chance to decide whether to continue with what we considered to be right or wrong, acceptable or unacceptable. Or adopt/adapt/drop down/pick up the new challenging idea or view to our long time held worldviews. This is an opportunity for the gospel communication and social and community intervention projects.

Christianity is just one of the world religions. As such, people need to see how better Christianity is compared to other world religions. Christians have a culture that is different from the cultures of other religions in Africa and elsewhere in the world. The most prevalent Christian and Muslim culture is its promotion of community life. Community life makes adherents of Christian and Islamic faith to develop interpersonal relationships and communicate with people effectively. It also helps members of the community to appreciate love, care and salvation.

Some important facts to consider in the anthropological culture concept are: *first*, no one culture is superior, holy, or inferior to any other.

3. Green, *Evangelism in the Early Church*, 76–78.

Second, no culture is full enough not to adapt into or adopt anything from another culture; whether for good or for bad. *Third*, no culture is exclusive of external or internal influences for change. There is always room for a change through adoption or adaptation of another culture anthropologically. These anthropological facts help a church planter or a missionary to look for an opportunity in any society for sharing the gospel with people of any culture and bring about change in the behavior of the people of the society.

ANTHROPOLOGICAL CULTURE CHANGE

I agree with Paul Hiebert and Charles Kraft that worldview is the locus for culture change. Though culture is dynamic and subject to change at any time, yet change may not be immediate. Worldview unifies a society in *what* and *how* they perceive work, believe, think and behave. As such, no individual decision may seriously be taken for culture change particularly in the non-western societies; and Africa in particular. Hence, the real factor for culture change is the worldview. The thinking patterns and power of imagination of the society are greatly influenced by their cultural worldview.

Since worldview is the heart of relationships in the society for development of cultural values, belief systems and motivation for work, its change is critical. Culture change in any society should significantly consider that necessity for change is for the people to turn to God and develop love for one another. Any process instituted for culture change ought to depend on the Holy Spirit guiding the process of change. We shall come back to the subject of culture change later in chapter 8 of this book. Charles Kraft mentioned two factors that bar culture change: Worldview barriers and Social barriers.

Paul Hiebert has mentioned the worldview as the factor that can bar culture change. I sincerely agree with both of them that worldview and socialization can adversely hinder culture change in any society. But I also assume that personal religious allegiances may also slow or hinder culture change entirely. Religion is a system of beliefs, rituals and values of a society or an individual about the deity. The relationship between religion and the society need critical study before implementing culture change. Understanding the relationship between religion and the society is important because it can help the cross-cultural minister to make the gospel relevant to the people of the society. "Before we can discuss the significance of any manifestation of religious change in a given society, we must understand how religion and the society relate."[4] The society as social and spiritual community in some cases, defines its worldview from these beliefs, rituals and values in terms of the conceptualized religion and the Supreme Being. Therefore, the study of how religion and worldview can bar society's cultural transformation is significant in both social development and spiritual transformation.

The controlling factor of the worldview in most Indian and other societies in Asia is the religion. Africa is no exception in this belief. The conceptualized religion controls the *whats* and *hows* of the society. In such cases, the zealots of the society's religion may compel others not to convert into any other religion, and as such, culture change by the gospel or social development may not be easy. The fact is culture change is possible. Every culture is subject to change at any time.

The question about culture change is centered on how different people perceive reality. The Western society assumes that the real world is made up of lifeless matter while the oriental people in Southeast Asia believe that the external world does not exist.

Individual people and the society change attitudes, beliefs and values when their reality has been challenged, reconstructed and perceived differently due to the acquisition and exposure to new knowledge. The difference certainly should make sense in contrast with the previous perceived reality. If the gospel is relevant to people's daily needs, culture change may be possible faster than otherwise.

One important thing that cross-cultural communicators need not to forget in culture change is the work of the Holy Spirit in the change process. The Holy Spirit deals with the heart and the soul of the individual people which is carnal and resistant to change. Once the heart and the soul are dealt with, change is inevitable. Sometimes the impact of change may not be immediate yet what is certain is that it is possible with the Holy Spirit and the gospel is the means to that effect.

Socialization can also hinder culture change. Social structure of the society is another factor worthy consideration when deciding for culture change in any society. The initiatives by nongovernmental organizations

4. Tippet, *Introduction to Missiology*, 157.

for culture change consider interpersonal relationships, status and peoples' roles in the society by emphasizing people's involvement in the social and community development activities. The coming of the gospel to change the society's worldview and religion is a threat to some statuses in the society as it was the case when the birth of Jesus Christ was announced. "Where is the one who has been born king of the Jews? We saw his star in the east and we have come to worship him. When King Herod heard this he was disturbed and all Jerusalem with him" (Matt 2:2–3). Herod and the people of Jerusalem were indignant and threatened upon hearing that a King of the Jews was born. Jesus Christ was not born King of the physically seen kingdom, yet Herod was threatened. Jesus' birth was not good news to Herod and his arrays. In this case study, we find that culture change can certainly be restrained if perceived a threat to the existing authority. Status matters in any society and to any people. Hence, needs critical study before instituting culture change. In Africa, status and roles are considered as personal achievements by some people, even Christians. This is why some leaders have adopted some titles to protect their positions. Any threat to status and role change in the society may receive stiff resistance for implementation. No one in Africa is ready to sacrifice his/her personal achievement for anything; be it the gospel or any other.

COMMUNICATION

Basically, in any communication the communicator aims at informing, persuading and convincing (seeking a response). In cross-cultural communication for example, the communicator (Missionary Preacher) aims at informing, persuading and convincing people that Jesus Christ is the Saviour and that he saves whoever believes in him. Therefore, the message must appeal to cognitive, affective and response to behavior change of the recipient (a cross-cultural listener). Communication has not taken place unless a response is achieved.[5]

"A sixth important contribution of anthropology to cross-cultural ministry is its focus on the elements of human behavior that relates to communication."[6] Communication is an important element to consider; both in social, and community development and evangelism programs for church planting activity. There is nothing that takes place in social

---

5. Phiri, *Cross-Cultural Communication: A Prototype Study Guide*, 4.

6. Charles Kraft, *Anthropology for Christian Witness*, 10.

life or evangelism that is not communication. In fact without communication, there is no evangelism or any human, social and community development.

In Social-Cultural Anthropology we focus our study on cultural relationships, governing beliefs, values and behaviors that affect communication of the gospel and community activities in the society. Good relationships the missionary or the social worker may develop with members of the society can enhance communication of the gospel in more effective way. In every society, people communicate in many ways including the silent language. Interpersonal relationship is for effective communication of the gospel at personal level. One of the African cultural values is interpersonal relationship. Africans value interpersonal relationship particularly because they are a community and oral people rather than individualistic and reading society. They depend on oral communication and face-to-face talk.

A church planter and a social community worker are automatically cross-cultural communicators; hence, understanding the culture of the society in which they work is significant. Every culture has its own means and symbols of communication. In Africa, most people use storytelling, riddles, parables and proverbs to communicate with each other. As an African and a participant observer I have always seen people in Africa using parables, proverbs, riddles and storytelling as means of communication. Every cross-cultural communicator should not take communication in a new culture, especially in Africa for granted. Even when a cross-cultural communicator is well vest with the language of the target community, communication should not be taken for granted. One can communicate effectively with Africans using storytelling as a strategy for gospel preaching and disseminating important information for social and community development. In fact, African ways of communication are similar to those of the ancient Israel. Their basic way of communication is oral through storytelling, artistic work like music, modeling and sculpting.

Communication also involves silent language that people use in their culture. A Cross-cultural communicator should not assume this language when he plans to communicate the gospel cross-culturally. Communication is more than using verbal or written language. Sometimes people express their emotions in gestures and other conventional symbols in their society.

Anthropologists do not assume communication with the people of different culture without understanding what it means to the immediate audience. *First*, they learn and understand the culture, form, meaning and symbols, even of silent language before presenting what they want to communicate. For example, a black suit may mean one thing in one society and it may mean something else in another society. *Second*, Social and Cultural anthropologists appreciate and respect the culture of the people they interact with before theorizing the beliefs of the society. Social workers and Missiologists may benefit a lot from these anthropological facts. Communication should therefore, be understood in the context of the culture of the respondent society. Missionaries should not come only to communicate what they want, but to integrate with the people they come to minister to or help to develop their social and community life.

Sometimes people reject the gospel not because it cannot save, but because the approach has no respect to the existing culture and the values of the society. Let me warn my fellow missionaries and social development workers that though culture is dynamic, it is not easily changed. Societies do not change culture at an overnight period. Cultural change takes time and consideration of other factors on which the society is established culturally. Therefore, social and community development workers and missionaries both need patience; which is the fruit of the spirit, to see change in the lives of people.

The gospel and social work must meet both the immediate and or future needs of the people in the society in order to insinuate cultural change effectively. This cannot be possible unless the society is holistically studied and needs identified; so that the gospel and the social development are directed toward those needs. Note that anthropology looks at the society holistically. Let people reject the gospel because they have understood it clearly, but they do not want to accept it for their own reasons; rather than people rejecting it because it has not been well communicated.

African values on personal relationships, face-to-face oral communication and event orientation may affect how communication is done cross-culturally. However, if the cross-cultural worker or church planter is aware of the impact of these values in Africa and anywhere else, communication may be enhanced significantly.

ANTHROPOLOGICAL RESEARCH METHODS

All research must begin with an accurately defined research question. The research question however, should be significant, realistic and measurable. "For research to take place there must be both a question to be answered and a system for knowledge acquisition and recording."[7]

Anthropology unlike other human and behavioral sciences it studies people through observation while incarnating in their culture. The anthropologist eats, celebrates, mourns and dwells with the people in their society. In fact, s/he becomes one like them in many aspects. This is why Jesus Christ incarnated in the Jewish culture. He was not a stranger to the Jewish culture in any way. Jesus Christ studied the Jewish culture and the peoples' faith in God, their cultural values, and what was considered to be the norms of Jewish culture and society. He became like one of them but not of the world. "What do people say the Son of Man is?" (Matt 16:13). "O unbelieving and perverse generation, how long shall I stay with you?" (Matt 17:17). Jesus asked these and many other enquiry questions to find out what people knew about him and their God. The responses that Jesus got from his disciples for these questions helped him to approach the Jewish society with much care. He communicated the gospel in very clear local language of the Jews. Through his simple research methodology of studying people while incarnating and staying with them helped him to identify their need of salvation; so he developed approaches that were easily understood by his audience. He gave illustrations and examples from the Jewish environment and culture. Communication was made simple and possible.

Jesus' method of research is what the missiological anthropologists have adopted. It was participatory action research method. He participated in their everyday life through incarnation and observation. Imagine Jesus celebrating with the people at the wedding at Cana! (John 2). Anthropology is similar and different from other social sciences because of its emphasis on holistic and incarnational approach to the subjects understudy. The researcher participates in the living situations of the subjects. He tastes their foods, lives in the homes like theirs, and feels what they feel. This is the strength of anthropology for social and community development workers, missionaries and church planters who want to impact the society with the gospel of the Kingdom and the social work. The method of ob-

7. Earl et al., *Conducting Research in the Practice setting*, 16.

serving *what* and *how* people think, eat, mourn, celebrate, dress, interact, and relate is very significant for anthropological researchers because it helps them understand the issues people go through and make the gospel and social development projects relevant to the society's needs. In fact, people do not just become subjects for study to the researcher in an anthropological study; but participant researchers.

A church planter who envisages church growth will certainly incarnate into his society's culture in order to win them to Christ just as Jesus did. Incarnation is already a research method for church planters and community development workers.

DATA COLLECTION AND ANALYSIS IN ANTHROPOLOGICAL STUDY

Anthropologists collect data through case studies, interviews, focus group discussions, observations and participatory action research. Usually, in anthropological research the data are in form of statements made by the subjects, literature reviews, recordings of critical phenomena observations and answers from the correctly and precisely asked questions. James Neil states that there are three main methods of data collection in qualitative research, which is interactive interviewing, written descriptions by participants and observation.[8]

The data collected through the means stated above are mainly subjective. Anthropological research is usually qualitative rather than quantitive. Therefore, precision in data analysis is not as it is in quantitative research where statistics are used and are objective. These data are analyzed through categorizing, critical contextualization and looking at similarities and differences of different scenarios, models and facts.

DISCUSSION QUESTIONS

- Read Acts 15:1–11. What was the question about in this portion of the scripture?
- How would you briefly analyze and address the question yourself?

---

8. Neil, *Analysis of Professional Literature*, para 4.

3

Incarnation and Interpersonal Relationships in Africa

- Introduction
- The Incarnation of Jesus Christ in the Jewish Culture
- The Incarnational Models for Cross-Cultural Workers
- Incarnation and Interpersonal Relationships

INTRODUCTION

THE THEOLOGY OF THE incarnation of Jesus Christ is a great challenge and a model of study to the twenty-first century church planter, social and community development worker, and the missionary. The Great Commission still stands, "Therefore *go* and *make* disciples of all nations . . . and *teaching* them to obey everything . . ." (Matt 28:19–20).

The first to obey the command of the Father was Jesus Christ himself who came and lived among us. Christ became like us-God with us (incarnation) (Matt 1:23). He became a servant, just like us (Phil 2:5–8). Unless we come to that humble state we can never incarnate into the respondent culture. Jesus' incarnation made him relevant to the Jewish society and the entire world he came to save. Through the incarnation process Jesus Christ understood the point of view of his Jewish society and perceived people as humans not just as souls.

Incarnational ministry requires that the minister, church planter, social and community worker, and a missionary be willing to be transformed through incarnation. Lingenfelter and Mayers suggest that missionaries should incarnate 100 percent into the culture of the people being reached with the gospel.[1] But the missionary should be careful

---

1. Lingenfelter and Mayers, *Ministering Cross-Culturally: An Incarnational Model for Personal Relationships,* 119.

that he or she should not compromise with Christian standards in the incarnation process. Some rituals which people practice in their societies are evil; thus, a missionary may not incarnate in them; such rituals as worshiping idols, chanting evil songs and cursing others.

The significance of incarnation ministry cannot be overemphasized. It is what Jesus Christ the Lord of Harvest has demonstrated its importance. It is the way of reconciling the lost to their Lord through observation and participation in the daily life challenges. It is one thing to live with people in their society; and it is another to incarnate in their culture for the sake of effective communication. Incarnation is adapting into the society's nature in terms of dressing mode, food, language and so forth. The cross-cultural communicator should identify himself/herself with the members of the society.

The Great Commission also holds that believers should teach everything that Jesus Christ taught them. Teaching involves knowing and understanding the students. Before teachers teach, first they understand the needs of the students. Teachers also teach by demonstration. They are required to teach by example. Students also learn by hearing and observing how their teachers live the talk. This is why it is important for the church planter to incarnate into the culture of his society so that he can understand what the members of the society are going through and eventually know how to preach to them. Unless there is intimate interaction and relationship with the society, communication may still be a problem to the church planter. The historian Luke said what Jesus began to do and teach (Acts 1:1). He referred to how Jesus communicated the gospel to people of his day. He humbled himself through incarnation. He taught what he did. His teaching was characterized by both theory and practice. Incarnation makes communication of the important information easy to the respondent society because both the missionary and the respondent society participate in what is happening. Therefore, social and community development worker, church planter, and the missionary need to incarnate into the respondent cultures in order to communicate the gospel and social development interventions effectively.

THE INCARNATION OF JESUS CHRIST
IN THE JEWISH CULTURE

Incarnation is the process of identifying oneself with the people and their culture by adapting into their culture. It may also be defined as a deliberate self-denial in order to accept, learn and understand the other person's worldview.

Cross-cultural ministry requires incarnation on the part of the minister and holistic approach in addressing issues affecting the society. The church planter and social development worker need to look at man holistically in any cultural setting just like Jesus Christ did. Jesus Christ perceived people as humans who had needs ranging from spiritual, psychological to social and physical. "People should be perceived as humans and not as souls."[2]

Philippians 2:6, 7 is the profound scripture to this effect. "Who, being in the very nature God . . . but made himself nothing taking the very nature of a servant." Jesus Christ stripped himself of heavenly attributes, language and body in order to incarnate into humanity, communicate and save a sinner. He humbled himself to the point that he was no different from a mere servant in Jewish society (John 13:13). Jesus' humility communicated the gospel to the people he ministered to in effective way because they saw him doing things that other teachers of the law did not do. He was born in a manger, grew up in a local Jewish home in Nazareth, and ate with local Jews. At one point he was likened to a publican. His dressing made no difference with any Jew. He was just like any other Jew in every respect in the Jewish society; a man who made difference in peoples' lives: the man, Jesus Christ. "In this respect, he was an ordinary child."[3] Because of incarnation and the holistic approach to the community he lived in, communication of the good news of the Kingdom to the Jews was not a problem. He knew and understood their culture and ultimate need.

Jesus Christ established relationships with the society leaders and the local Jews (John 3:2). He celebrated with those who were celebrating, "And Jesus and his disciples had also been invited to the wedding" (John 2:2). When people needed his help they approached him without hesitation. They asked him for wine; he gave them for free. He healed those who needed healing. He interacted with them in many forums including worship services (Luke 2:41–47). He mourned with those who mourned, "Jesus wept" (John 11:35). He became a real man in that society that no one would doubt his being one of them. In this Incarnational model,

2. Newberry, "PowerPoint presentation" *Master of Arts: Cultural Anthropology Class.*

3. Lingenfelter and Mayers, *Ministering Cross-Culturally: An Incarnational Models for Personal Relationships,* 16.

communicating the gospel to the people of that society would certainly not be a problem. Jesus Christ demonstrated the life worthy emulation by the church planter and any missionary who wants to impact and engages in cross-cultural communication ministry in Africa.

In Africa, people relate well with people who live, eat and participate in their cultural activities. Africans are people oriented because of their background in extended family relations, communal life and face to face oral communication. Africans are unique in their relationship with people who are considered strangers or foreigners. They interact easily with foreigners who are friendly. Therefore, incarnation in the African culture can certainly help the missionary and any social development worker communicate effectively.

THE INCARNATIONAL MODELS
FOR CROSS-CULTURAL WORKERS

There are two biblical models of incarnation. The first model is of Jesus Christ and the second one is of Apostle Paul. Jesus Christ became man in every aspects of humanity except in sin. He identified himself with humanity and the Jewish culture and the society in which he was born and grew up. The community recognized him as the son of Joseph, the carpenter. Yet, Jesus Christ made significant revolution in people's lives. No man in Israel made an impact in people's lives both spiritually and socially more than Jesus did.

The second model is of the Apostle Paul. Paul the apostle was a Jew and called to be an apostle to the gentiles; but preached the gospel to both the Jews and the gentiles. He personally incarnated into every culture of the people he preached to and made such an impact for Christ. He became everything to every people (1 Cor 9:19–23).

The gospel though important and significant as it is, will not be relevant and make any impact to any people, unless incarnated into the culture of the respondent society. Just as Jesus Christ became relevant to the Jewish society through incarnation, and Apostle Paul to the gentiles; so should the church planter and a missionary be in Africa. Africans love and associate easily with people who appreciate their culture more than the one who criticizes it. "The significant fact about the incarnation is that Jesus was a learner. He was not born with knowledge of language or culture."[4] As is the case with all anthropological studies, Jesus Christ

4. Ibid, 16.

studied and learnt the beliefs, values, rituals, language and culture of his immediate society in order to communicate the message of salvation. He did not bring into the world from heaven the language or culture. In other words, both Jesus Christ and the Apostle Paul became students of their own society's cultural, economic and social environment. They also learned and adapted belief and value systems, culture, language, food, ethics, and morals of their immediate societies. A church planter ought not to import his culture into the mission field. He should become a learner of his immediate society's environment if he wants missiological impact in the respondent society.

The missionary or the social and community development worker in Africa needs to relate with the respondent society first through incarnation before s/he communicates the gospel or any social development intervention. Many social development interventions have failed in Africa because there is always a communication gap existing between the donors and the African implementers.

Actually, Africans are noncrisis oriented people. As is the case of noncrisis oriented people; they are not time conscious. So, many Africans oftentimes do not meet deadlines of the assignments unless such assignments are reinforced positively in some way. This is from personal experience in working with Africans as the head teacher, lecturer and pastor.

Figure 1: *Incarnational Model for Effective Cross-Cultural Communication.*

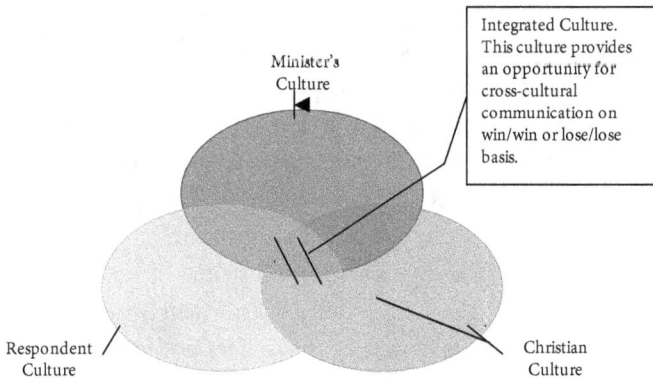

In this model, the three concentric circles represent three different cultures. The purple concentric circle stands for the Cross-Cultural Minister's culture, the yellow concentric circle stands for the culture of the respondent society and the sky blue concentric circle stands for the Christian culture. The respondent society and the minister must lose some of their best cultural biases, prejudices, values, and beliefs such as food recipes, dressing mode and language so as to integrate with the Christian and the respondent culture through incarnation, interpersonal relationships and then, change the behavior of the respondent community. If integrated culture can be achieved, gospel communication in Africa may be possible also. The Christian culture is the controlling culture in this model because it bases its values and belief systems on the Holy Spirit and biblical principles. The integration of minister's culture, respondent's culture, which is an African culture in this study and Christian culture which is basically biblical culture prepares the premise for sharing the gospel with the cross-cultural society with minimum communication problems. The integrated culture is formed by the interaction of all three cultures in the model. This allows any of the cultures to adopt, adapt and accommodate each other. The integrated or interactive culture is the one that creates the interaction and interrelationships of the three cultural worldviews; the cross-cultural minister's culture, the respondent culture and Christian culture. The cross-cultural minister is responsible to create the integrated culture by developing relationships with the local members of the society and making Christianity relevant to the society by living it. S/he should show interest in becoming a friend and a learner of the new culture, language, beliefs and values of the invaded society. In the integrated culture and worldview, gospel communication can be possible. In fact at this stage of incarnation, the cross-cultural minister will have acquired enough language skills, understanding of value and belief systems of the society in which he is a minister.

The Cross-Cultural Minister will be able to understand the thinking patterns, value systems, and perceptual reality just like his immediate society. The religion of the cross-cultural minister will not be perceived as a threat to the existing belief system of the society nor foreign to the people he has incarnated into. Each of the three variables in the model will be ready to accommodate each other and share common values, beliefs and worldviews for culture change and ease communication with the members of the target society. In Africa, this is practically possible because most Africans relate well with people who show interest in learning their culture. Most importantly, incarnation leads people to develop interest in each other. Since Africans live as a family in their communities, gospel communication and social development interventions may be effective.

The cross-cultural minister can incarnate into the African culture if he considers the people in the society he reaches with the gospel that they are people just like him/her. He should free himself from his cultural biases and prejudices about the African society. We observed in the previous chapter that there is no superior or inferior, holy or unholy culture. No culture is holy by itself. Jesus Christ wants all people to the ends of the earth to align their cultures, beliefs and values with God of the nations. In Christianity, the truth and absolute reality is the Lord God of the nations. This is the object of the whole incarnational process in Social-Cultural Anthropology. The unique strength of Africans in incarnation is that they are easily attracted to people who have interest in learning their culture, language and beliefs. Thus, they make themselves available to help the learner; learn and understand their culture.

INCARNATION AND INTERPERSONAL RELATIONSHIPS

People from various cultural backgrounds have different beliefs and value systems. Africans also have unique beliefs, food recipes and cultural dressing that is different from the Western perspective. Because of this concept, conflicts are inevitable in all intercultural relationships. The distance you can go along with the African depends on how patient you can be with him or her when she or he annoys you most with his illiteracy, unique food stuffs, cultural beliefs and so forth. Jesus Christ might have persevered the actions, beliefs, ignorance and values of his disciples and the Jews of his days. Patience is the fruit of the Holy Spirit (Gal 5:22) that ought to be cultivated in the life of a cross-cultural minister who wants to incarnate into the African culture; yet to grow in that fruit is by grace of the Lord. Most of us are not patient enough to wait until we understand why things are done this way or that way and why people behave in this way in the foreign cultural society. We would want things change at our pace not at the pace of the respondent society. Africans are generally slow to changes because of community-orientation and consultative decision making; therefore, the incarnating minister or social development worker needs to cultivate the fruit of patience in her or him, otherwise change may not be obtained as expected.

On the other hand, social and community development workers, missionaries and sending churches would want to see the fruits of their work or investment within the shortest time they can wait. Probably such time may be two years to a maximum of three years to some. If nothing encouraging is reported within this timeframe, they consider the mission to have been failed; yet, developing relationships with people who are of different culture, thinking patterns, beliefs and value systems is not easy, however. It requires patience.

Incarnational ministry to people who are not born in the society they reach out for Christ requires long lasting patience. For the cross-cultural minister to develop relationships with Africans is not an easy endeavor either. It requires that the minister be patient and be a keen learner of the already existing interpersonal relationships in the society. Between the cross-cultural minister and the respondent society there is cultural conflict, worldview conflict, value system conflict etc. "To become incarnate in any culture, we must learn to adapt to it."[5] Adaptation to the African foods, thinking patterns, rituals and values is the responsibility of a cross-cultural minister. However, such an adaptation is not at his finger tips either. Patience is the only fruit of the Holy Spirit that can bring it to pass. But adaptation into another culture is possible and significant element for incarnation ministry; particularly in Africa. "If we are to minister successfully to the members of a different society, therefore, we must learn about and participate in their culture."[6] Learning is a process that requires patience for change to manifest. The learning process in the incarnation ministry takes place in both the cross-cultural minister and in the people of the society he/she lives among. The people also learn how the minister interacts with them whether he/she is friendly or not. The way, the minister treats the beliefs, values, food and language; of the Africans matter most in the learning process of the people of his/her present society.

Generally, it is easy to make friendship with and learn from a person who relates well with other people. A cross-cultural minister and the social development worker should be people oriented. They ought to

5. Ibid, 118.
6. Ibid, 120.

develop interpersonal relationships with the indigenous people before sharing with them the gospel and any material things. Through these interpersonal relationships he or she can make the indigenous people his/her teachers as s/he learns their language and other cultural beliefs. In addition, good interpersonal relationships can open several opportunities for gospel communication and social interventions in any society in Africa.

Incarnation is the process of adapting into the culture of the people with whom you live and work. A cross-cultural minister ought to incarnate into the culture of the people he intends to reach with the gospel. However, the process of incarnation is not an easy one. *First*, the cross-cultural minister should take away his/her prejudices about the culture of the people he dwells among. S/he should accept them as they are in their cultural setting. This is exactly what Jesus Christ did with the Jews. He accepted the Jews and their culture as they were and adapted in that society. *Second*, after adapting in the society, the cross-cultural minister should study and know the people whose culture s/he has adapted. This is very important because every society has values and beliefs that have established that society and formed their worldview. "There is no way to properly relate to people of a totally different culture from one's own except by taking real effort to study and know people."[7] Basically, missions is about relating with people while sharing with them the message of salvation in addressing their spiritual, social and physical needs. Therefore, incarnation requires the cross-cultural minister to develop relationships while incarnating into the African society.

Learning the African culture helps the missionary and the social development worker to remove barriers in communication, to recognize and use the tools of relationship, to understand the importance of form and meaning in communication, and to be able to relate cultural relativism and biblical absolutism in cross-cultural ministry.[8]

Third, to incarnate into the African culture, a cross-cultural minister and the social development worker needs thorough study of the society's social structure, religion and their impact on peoples' thinking patterns, behaviours, beliefs and value systems.

---

7. Clement et al., *Cross-Cultural Christianity: A Text Book in Cross-Cultural Communication*, 29.

8. Reed, *Preparing Missionaries: For Intercultural Communication*, 79.

An African society is an institution bound with and established on ethics, morals and laws that are unique to their culture in determining its worldview. A cross-cultural minister should not take this institution for granted. The norms of African society are unique to Africans. Of course, in sociology there is what is called universal culture. But African norms are distinctive to African society. As such, the norms of the African society should not be taken for granted in the social development work, Incarnational Ministry and gospel communication. They need thorough study and understanding to interpret them effectively in African context.

In most African societies, religious syncretism, extended families, cohabitation marriages, burying the dead without postmortem, oral communication and so forth are considered society norms. Extended families, speaking through a representative person to elders when you are wrong, respect for the elders and so forth have values in the African society. Therefore, any missionary or social development worker who overlooks these norms and values may find it difficult to communicate effectively with this society. Africans are knitted together as a society through integration of these and other rituals, beliefs and values.

Africans are very religious. Almost in every African community people have one common religion or they syncretize in their religious worship. It is important to understand these things when working among African societies. Africans incarnate into any cultural systems very easily because they usually take incarnation as an adventure. This is why religious syncretism is common in Africa.

DISCUSSION QUESTIONS

- Discuss the relationship between incarnation and interpersonal relationships
- How can you develop an effective incarnational model for cross-cultural communication?
- Describe the incarnational models of Jesus Christ and the apostle Paul as laid down in the Bible.

4

Ethnographic Aspects of the African Society

- Introduction
- The Society and the Social Structure
- Definitions
- Organization of the African Society
- The Societal Impact on the Church Growth
- Discussion Questions

INTRODUCTION

E VERY SOCIETY IS MADE up of ethnic groups. These ethnic groups have cultures that are identities of their societies. Now, the challenges of Missions and social development of the African societies in the twenty-first century are; first, reaching the ethnic or linguistic groups that have not accessed the gospel. Patrick Johnstone and Mandryk states that missions in the twenty-first century ought to list unreached peoples either as ethno-lingual, ethno-cultural or both.[1] Somalia, Mauritania, Tunisia, Morocco and Algeria are the African countries politically and religiously restricted to the gospel. Christianity in these countries is currently at less than one per cent; yet the total population of these countries by 2010 will approximately be one hundred million.[2]

Although Johnstone and Mandryk consider ethnicity and language to be the major hindrances of the majority population to the gospel; yet religion and political restrictions still have greater impact on gospel communication in non Christian oriented countries. In Africa, people from

1. Johnstone and Mandryk, *Operation World*, 225–26.
2. Ibid, 41.

other countries can enter into any country and learn any language they want. But if people in the community the missionaries have gone into already have a religion and political leadership that does not tolerate other religions, it becomes difficult for the missionaries to preach the gospel. This is why there are religious persecutions for the missionaries in some countries in Africa; such as Sudan, Nigeria, Somalia, Algeria, and so forth. It is true that the unfinished work is among the people groups that are engulfed in the culture or linguistic identities. However, it should not be ruled out that religion and politics do not have influence on their social structures and communication systems. These people groups have social structures and communication systems influenced culturally, religiously and politically that need critical exploration and study.

Western nations have influenced African states greatly culturally, politically and socio-economically. Some of these influences have been conceptualized in African cultures without adequate understanding and knowledge about them. As such, application of such theories from the West has affected how people need to relate to each other; since Africans are oral and community oriented society. Hence, the purpose of this chapter is to briefly study the Western influence on the organization of African society and develop information for cross-cultural Church Planter and the social and community development worker in the Africa society.

THE SOCIETY AND THE SOCIAL STRUCTURE

Ethnographically, the kinship influences the social structure of the African society distinct to other societies in the world. In Africa, societies are organized ethnically in kingdoms and nations under political powers. Paul Hiebert categorizes societies into tribal, peasant and urban societies.[3] The African society has social structure to categorize people of the community into statuses and roles in their tribes, clans and villages. Socio-economically, for example in Malawi, Zambia and Zimbabwe, the societies are categorized and organized into Village Development Committees (VDC), Area Development Committees (ADC) and District Development Committee (DDC).[4] These social structures enhance social and human development of the society in the

---

3. Hiebert, "Social Structure and Church Growth," 426.

4. Lenneiye, *Quest for Corporate Leadership: Public Case Studies for Southern Africa,* 144.

country. Development plans of the country have wider participation and consultations because of these structures. However, the functions of the societies depend on the role the people and their leaders play according to their social category in the society. For example, the head of the VDC is the Village Head, ADC is headed by the Senior Chief and the District Commissioner chairs the DDC. These are key leaders in social and community development of the African society.[5] Therefore, when planning to preach the gospel and do social and community development work in African society, the missionary and the social development worker should understand the roles of these offices.

In Social-Cultural Anthropology, it is important to recognize the social category of people which is sociologically called social structure. In Africa, people love to be recognized by the statuses they hold in a society. Consequently, this affects the way people relate and communicate in that particular society. In most African societies, respect of the elders and people with special recognition in the society comes first before communication of the important information for the benefit of the society. The issue of "All protocol observed" does not go well with the African culture of recognizing ranks and file. Every person in Africa wants special or personal recognition.

Within a society there are subcultures that influence small communities within bigger communities. This is an indication that there is always communication taking place between people in the society.

In this chapter, we will study the definitions of society, social structures, society organization and its impact on church growth and social and community development.

In Africa, most societies are categorized as urban or rural depending on social and economic development of those societies. The communication channels, language and media vary from urban to rural societies.

DEFINITIONS

What is a society any way? What about social structures? Do social structures matter in missions, church planting and social and community development?

History of missions clearly indicates that Missions is interdisciplinary course of study. The contributions of Social Sciences to missions have

5. Ibid, 144.

been quite significant and appreciated by missionaries particularly in the twentieth century. It is the expectation of the missiological anthropologists that this will be so even in the twenty-first century.

Paul Hiebert defines a society as "a group of people who relate to one another in orderly ways in different settings."[6] People in a society relate to one another culturally, ethnically and sometimes linguistically; and communication follows the same channels. Richard Schaefer defines a society as "A fairly large number of people who live in the same territory, are relatively independent of people outside it, and participate in a common culture".[7] A society is a group of people who have the same or similar cultural practices, generally have the common languages and transmit it to the next generation within the society as a norm of life. The common cultural practices and languages make interrelationships possible and easy in a society. Members of the society easily understand each other and usually they take form and meaning for granted and unconsciously. This belief provides easy channels of communication in any society. The cross-cultural communicator should therefore take advantage of these channels to enhance communication of the gospel and concepts of social development.

Social structure is the way in which a society is organized into predictable relationships.[8] The relationships of people in a society depend on the interaction of people between the social classes or categories in which they are recognized in that particular society. Members of the society are recognized according to statuses and roles they play in the society. Paul Hiebert defined status as "a position in a social system occupied by individuals".[9] In a caste system, for example, people who belong to a higher caste are considered significant by their positions in the Hindu religion and society. The higher caste controls the economy and political power of the society. Therefore, relationship in that society is certainly determined by the higher or upper class of people. The role played by people in the higher caste sets the standard to be followed by the lower castes; though this is now changing due to cultural dynamics, political pluralism, and religious diversity, social and economic develop-

---

6. Hiebert, *Anthropological Insights for Missionaries*, 51.

7. Schaefer, *Sociology*, 58.

8. Ibid, 103.

9. Hiebert, "Social Structure and Church Growth", 423.

ment. As observed by Hiebert in Ralph Winter and Steven Hawthorne that Church growth faces caste discrimination in India. Caste system is a hindrance to church growth not because people are not saved, but the level of caste to which a particular person belongs limits that person to associate with members of the society from another caste.[10] Therefore, church planters in that kind of society face a challenge of either planting a church for each caste or choose otherwise.

In Africa, social discrimination depends on whether a person belongs to a royal family or not. People from the royal family receive special respect and they are expected to behave well. People in a society play several roles according to their statuses. The roles played by individuals contribute more significantly to the interactions of people and how that society develops spiritually, socially and economically. And relationships depend on the integration of roles of various people holding different positions in the society and their respect to gender and age. In fact, people depend on one another in the African society for the roles played by others. In cross-cultural ministry, it is important to consider individuals' status and roles more critically as they relate to the African culture and communication networks within and outside the society.

A role is a function a person performs in a society to contribute to its spiritual welfare and socio-economic development of the society. People with various statuses play several roles in a society to build relationships among its members and develop the spiritual and social emerging leaders of the society. Hence, the African society is bonded with interpersonal relationships and roles played by individuals and the community. Each member of the society is expected to contribute to the welfare and development of the society by playing a spiritual, economical, political and social role. The church should provide a forum for these roles to be played by members of the church or the society.

ORGANIZATION OF THE AFRICAN SOCIETY

1. Organization of Statuses and Roles

The African society is organized in terms of statuses and roles of the members of the society. It is also socially structured into extended families, tribes, clans, villages and so forth. And the statuses and roles are held

10. Winter and Hawthorne, *Perspectives: On the World Christian Movement*, 422.

and played by the presidents, kings, village chiefs, and heads of tribes, clans, family heads and individual members of the society.

Kings and village heads are enthroned following culturally accepted means. The culturally accepted means of appointing and instating chiefs and kings in Africa follows the lineage in the royal family. Kings and chiefs are born and never made. People dance and play music to show their happiness and to communicate the social and spiritual ideals of the society when enthroning chiefs and kings in Africa. This is certainly distinct from the way kings are enthroned elsewhere in the world. Apart from kings and chiefs, all other society leaders are made through election and training systems.

Kings and chiefs in Africa have power to hear cases between opposing parties just as the court does in other societies outside Africa. They punish the offender and acquit the innocent. The punishments imposed on the offender depend on the gravity of the case; which defines the norms the offender has broken. For example, marrying someone's wife may result in the offender paying for the damage equivalent to the bride price to the husband. While encroaching in someone's field or plot may result in paying a goat to the chief or king because in Africa the land belongs to kings and chiefs. People who are prosecuted by the chiefs or kings are considered to have violated the most important norms of the societies. In the American societies these norms would be called Mores (pronounced *mor-ays*).[11]

Africans are not formal in conducting meetings. They may call for a meeting under the tree as long as the quorum is reached. Usually, traditional meetings whether they are court proceedings or any other meetings, there are no minutes recorded and take place in the open ground under the tree rather than in the confines. The missionary or social worker may take the minutes if s/he needs them. What matters in Africa is whether the meeting took place. In Africa, a quorum is more important than time because of communalism. The presence of the chief or the king and two contending parties suffices to proceed with the court deliberations only if there are witnesses and observers. Unless it is critically important to have other community leaders, the proceedings may not be suspended. No one asks for minutes in traditional African

---

11. Schaefer, *Sociology*, 66.

meetings. This is a clear indication that Africans are oral, informal and communal societies.

Members of the African society have statuses and roles to play for the welfare of their society. "In our society, formal organizations fulfill an enormous variety of personal and societal needs and shape the lives of every one of us".[12] In Africa, formalization of the society organization is not considered as necessary. Every society has people who have certain statuses. For example, a Missionary, General Superintendent, President, Village Chief, General Manager, Managing Director, Chief Executive etcetera. The statuses of these positional leaders give them mandate to control and exercise authority in the society for which they are leaders. The relationship of some of these leaders to other members of the society is a *Master-Servant*. This relationship is detrimental to gospel communication cross-culturally; yet most African church and other society leaders consider themselves as masters. They expect the society members to serve them instead of the leaders serving the society. A manager, missionary or General Superintendent is *not a master* to the people in any society he is working. *S/he is a servant-leader* leading and serving other servants. They are both servants of the Most High God. The status one occupies in the society can be used for good or abused depending on how s/he views herself/himself in relation to other members of the society. In servant-leadership the leader serves rather than being served. *Servant-leadership* is what Jesus Christ, the Chief Shepherd demonstrated as a model for Christian leaders (John 13:1–17). *Servant-leadership* is more than just a status in its impact for church growth and social and community development. There is less expression of servant-leadership among African leaders. Most African leaders are power hungry. This is one reason why there are so many political conflicts on the continent of Africa. The character of servant-leadership can hardly be found in most of the African leaders who are power hungry. The desire for higher status and servanthood do not usually go together. Servant-leadership calls for humility which is a rare characteristic for most political and church leaders in Africa.

The status in the church and at social work place should be occupied with an attitude of serving the purposes and needs of others and God rather than of your own interest (Phil 2:3–4). The roles the social devel-

---

12. Ibid, 132.

opment worker, missionary or church planter should play in any society should be of serving others in love and humility rather than expecting others to serve him. The role of a member of the society should be to contribute to the welfare of the total society holistically.

The African society is communal in nature and as it is the case with all oral societies, communication is face to face talk. Africans also communicate through music and dances. Members of the African society are bonded together in decision-making, worldview and respond to situations affecting their spiritual, social and economic lives as a community. However, this also depends on their statuses and roles in that society.

Membership in African societies is involuntary. People become members of the society by birth. They communicate through oral traditions, music and traditional dances; while the Westerners use literatures and mass media for communication.

In a church planting endeavour, it is imperative for the cross-cultural minister to understand the statuses and roles played in the organization of the society. The cross-cultural minister and the African nationals have different statuses and roles in the society when preaching the gospel. Both the cross-cultural minister and the African nationals are important and responsible to organize their work in accordance with God and the society's expectation.

Every society has specific expectation of the missionary and social development worker; whether the expectations are based on presumptions or realities. These expectations challenge the cross-cultural minister in Africa to demonstrate Christ-like character and servanthood both in communicating the gospel and social interventions to the local members of the society. In the African setting, the missionary is expected to be a white person with a lot of wealth and drives an expensive vehicle; though this concept is now diminishing because many Africans are now becoming missionaries and they do not have the facilities enjoyed by the Western missionaries; yet they are recognized as missionaries. The social worker is always thought to be a person who is sponsored or funded by Western donors. In most African societies, the donation is understood as their money which should be distributed freely to the society members.

2. Institutional Organization

Institutionally, the African society is organized in terms of families, tribes, clans, kingdoms, civil governments and courts. However, due to dynamism of social and political structures, Africa has also been developed and organized into countries, regions, civil governments and so forth. The chiefs, kings and recognized political leadership, legal courts play different roles in the welfare of the African society. For example, they hear and settle illegal social issues in the society, provide spiritual and social support for the needy. The courts, chiefs and kings sort out most deviant behaviours in the society. The illegal social issues that would be heard at the competent court in the United States of America or any country in the West are sometimes heard at the chief's court. Africans have their unique way of looking at issues legally, socially and economically. In fact, death sentence in Africa came as a result of social development from well developed Western legal systems. The equivalent punishment of death sentence in Africa would probably be forty lashes or so.

In African culture, the extended family relations like uncles and aunties would take responsibility of looking after orphans. In traditional African culture, the terms 'orphan or orphanage' are strange. People perhaps never used this term to describe a child left by a dead relative because they were considered discriminatory. In Africa, no one has one mother or father. Sisters to your mother are your mothers; and all brothers to your father are your fathers. So, if your biological father or mother has died, the immediate brother or sister to your father or mother would take care of you without any complaint. In fact, there are people who grew up without knowing that their biological parents died when they were young. People would take care of each other without seeking funds for supporting orphans in their locality. No one would love to see the son or daughter of his/her relative on the street as a street kid. Africans learned to take care of each other's children. However, this does not mean supporting orphans is wrong as it is done today. But most Africans did not know the term orphan the way it is known in the contemporary world. It is sad that the family institutions in Africa have withdrawn their support to the orphans as it used to be in the African society. Of course this is due to economic challenges facing the extended families.

In African society, any social problem, be it funeral or sickness, famine or any other is always considered a communal problem. Africans bear each other's burdens because they are a community and perceive the world as a village of the related people group with the similar needs. Therefore, social development workers ought to understand how African society is organized. People in Africa have communal perception of reality and relationships. As a result, communication of the gospel and social intervention programs need to consider how people in this society are related to each other and view their world.

THE SOCIETAL IMPACT ON CHURCH GROWTH

The way the society is organized can significantly affect the communication of the gospel for the church growth. According to the assessment of Paul Hiebert, the growth of the church depends on whether the society is a tribal, peasant or urban. Each society will demand its own approach because it has its own challenges to church planting or church growth. Each of the society has its own characteristics that makes it unique; and thus, demand a particular approach for gospel presentation. The following are the characteristics of each society according to Paul Hiebert (1999) in *Perspectives*:

1. Tribal Societies
    - Has stress on kinship as basis for social bonding
    - Strong group orientation with mutual responsibility and group decision-making process
    - Minimal social hierarchy
    - Vertical communication[13]

In this type of society, no individual decision should be taken seriously unless there is sign of genuine repentance in the convert. Group decision is final and concrete. In this kind of society, the absolutes of the society are final and established; no matter how one person perceives them. If the society feels threatened by the change they may reject it. Usually what works in such type of societies is the "majority and elderly must rule." Parents and other elderly personalities in the society have always a say on what the younger generation or an individual has decided. Most African societies have tribal characteristics. Therefore, communication in Africa needs to consider how communalism and kinship can affect the preaching of the gospel and the implementation of the social development work.

13. Hiebert, "Social Structure and Church Growth", 425.

2. Peasant Societies

- Has stress on kinship as basis for social bonding
- Strong group orientation with group decision-making process
- Intergroup hierarchs
- Communicate horizontally within groups, vertically between them.[14]

In this cultural setting, each group needs special attention. Caste systems fall in this category of the society. For church growth, each group should be attended to separately because it is unique; until such a time when they will understand that they are one in Christ. Jesus Christ is Lord of all (Rom 10:12–13). Each group may need a church planted in their society because they cannot fellowship with people from the other caste or class freely. In this case, growth can be determined by the size of the population of the caste or class of people in that society.

3. The Urban Societies

- Has stress on individualism and personal decision-making
- Organizations on basis of voluntary associations, networks and geographic groupings
- Heterogenents and hierarchs
- Use of mass media in addition to networks.[15]

The evangelistic and discipleship methods for this kind of society are diverse. This society needs frequent updates of information because technological changes in the cities are fast and influence daily decisions. In this society, people change friendships and relationships quite often. People move to various places for job or business opportunities more often as well. Church growth in the urban society is hectic and challenging because people come and go very unexpectedly. In fact, it is even difficult to designate membership in some cases. The church becomes a fellowship of convenience.

The urban society is the most complicated one for both evangelistic strategy and discipleship. Time for fellowship service on Sundays

14. Ibid, 426–27.
15. Ibid, 428.

is the most strenuous one. In this situation, the pastor needs to be very organized, strategic, innovative and flexible because changes might occur at a time he did not expect. The numerical and financial growth can be both deceptive and frustrating sometimes. People in the urban communities have networking relationships; and they communicate through their networks. Michael McGriff said "Blessed are the flexible, for they shall not be bent out of shape."[16] The urban society is unstable because of constant changing urban environment due to political and economic challenges. The cross-cultural minister and the social development worker should be flexible in planning his/her ministry in the urban society.

The growth of the church depends on the organization of the society and effectiveness of the communication strategy. Ray Bakke declares that churches are the products of culture and history, and all kinds are likely found in large cities.[17] The tribal society which applies well to the Africans can haphazardly affect the growth of the church if not critically studied. Africans communicate orally; although literacy levels have increased tremendously in Africa in the twenty-first century. Reading culture is not yet developed among most Africans. Hence, traditional oral communication needs to be held and develop a transitional strategy into a reading culture and literature communication. Most Africans would tell you that they forgot to reply to a letter or read it. What they actually mean is that they did not read it. Currently, Africans should be understood as oral communicators. They still value face to face talk and personal presence as means of communication in their society. Africans are communal and oral communicators. Communal decisions and vertical communication carry much weight than personal or individual ones. They have respect of elders' decisions. Africans are consultative in decision making. This is the strength of the African society in terms of decision making. The decision of an African in most cases is a contribution of the entire community.

16. McGriff, In *The 17 Essential Qualities of a Team Player: Becoming the Kind of Person Every Team Wants*, 1.

17. Bakke, *The Urban Christian: Effective Ministry in Today's Urban World*, 17.

DISCUSSION QUESTIONS

- Discuss the African ethnographic social structure and how it can enhance spiritual and social development of the society.
- How does Paul Hiebert define social structure?
- Explain the organization of African society institutionally and organizationally.

5

Social Interaction and Reality in Africa

- Introduction
- Definition of Reality
- Reality from Humanistic Perspective
- Reality from God's Perspective
- Social Interaction and Reality
- Discussion Questions

INTRODUCTION

Social-Cultural Anthropology is about interpersonal relationships, behavior, and communication in a society for spiritual, social and economic development of the society. There are always interactions between people in any society that influence their worldviews and behavior. As they interact, they share their common views in the process through their relationship networks. This is communication. One of the basic views they share is the perceptual reality. Like I said earlier on in the previous chapter, reality is relative from humanistic view point. People perceive reality from the definition of their cultural worldview. Is there any room for absolute or objective reality?

In Social-Cultural Anthropology, our purpose is to study the cultural relationships, belief systems and communication in the African society for establishing absolute reality, effective gospel communication and social development work in Africa.

In social interactions and reality, we find that people define reality in various ways. But in this chapter, our definition will be limited to cross-cultural missionary and social development worker in Africa and God's perspective of reality.

DEFINITION OF REALITY

The study of reality is philosophical because people in any society have different perception or point of view about the world, themselves, and other people. Reality defines what and how people know what they know and believe what they believe. A cross-cultural missionary and a social development worker are no exception of such perceptions. What seems real in the perception of a cross-cultural missionary may not be so in the respondent culture because human perception is subjective. Therefore, the study of reality is critical in cross-cultural communication of the gospel and social development work.

Reality cannot be taken for granted in a foreign culture. Reality is defined in terms of form and meaning derived from worldview of the society. This is why studying reality from both humanistic and God's perspective is significant.

In defining the term, reality, let me begin with a story about the Israelites. Why Joshua and Caleb had different description of what they saw in Canaan from the other ten Israelites whom Moses sent to spy the land of Canaan? Why the four authors of the gospel accounts differ in their writing of the story about Jesus Christ; yet they all describe the same subject and situation? And who had the right description? Finally what is the premise of determining who is right or wrong, and what is right or wrong? These and many other questions are quite difficult to answer in one word or so. Therefore, reality is not an easy concept to define; nevertheless, it is possible to define.

Reality is defined in the perception and evaluation of the whole. Whatever we see is partial and it is real only to the observer's point of view. With the finite mind and other human limitations, it is impossible to conceptualize the whole picture and interpret it as real. However, the observer's view point of anything is real to him or her. God, the creator of the world knows the reality of it all.

I would also like to concur with Kraft that there is objective reality and subjective reality.[1] Reality interpreted at the observer's point of view is subjective because it does not conceptualize the whole world. The reality of the world at God's perception is objective because he looks at the whole picture. Nevertheless, the world we look at is real and concrete.

1. Charles Kraft, *Anthropology for Christian Witness*, 18.

REALITY FROM HUMANISTIC PERSPECTIVE

Reality from humanistic perspective is subjective. Every person describes just one side of the whole picture according to his or her perception. Stephen Neil says there is no mind that can comprehend and definitively get the whole portrait of the gospel.[2] That is true for many Africans today. This implies that people perceive things in their societies differently and come up with different conclusions of the whole. Africa as a society develops its reality from its cultural worldview and makes conclusions depending on what their worldview defines the concepts realistically. The African cultural worldview is such that no one lives to himself or herself. Every person belongs to another in a community. This reality is also subjective. The whole African society just perceives a part of the whole picture according to lenses of their cultural background, learning and development. Africans in their society interpret events, issues, language through these lenses. The way Africans interpret reality in a society determines: first, *what* and *how* time is set, when certain events should be held and why. Second, it signals what they can believe and how they can communicate basic beliefs and values to other people in their society. Hence, African humanistic reality is subjective and is distorted due to the partiality of the definition and description of the total whole.

REALITY FROM GOD'S PERSPECTIVE

God as the creator of the world has the whole world in perspective. God has the reality of the whole world. In fact it is his. He knows the beginning and the end of everything on earth and in heaven. Therefore the reality according to God is objective. His interpretation of the events, time, and etcetera demonstrates his omniscience of everything he has created.

When preaching the gospel cross-culturally, it should be understood that reality of sin, salvation, eternal life, and eternal destruction is subjective to the cross-cultural society. The way people perceive their reality helps them to define words, concepts, and ideas differently from the presenter of the message. In God's perception, reality is objective and concrete. Therefore, when he says he will save those who believe in Jesus Christ and condemn those who will not believe he just means that. It

2. Neil, *Jesus through Many Eyes,* 64.

is imperative therefore for the cross-cultural minister to understand the reality of the respondent society in God's perception.

SOCIAL INTERACTION AND REALITY

People in a society interact socially whether for good or bad. For example, deviant behaviour is the influence of social interaction with people of evil mindset. People's minds are informed through interaction with knowledge learned from other people and their way of life.

When Moses sent twelve spies to spy the land of Canaan, we observe that there was interaction between the spies and the Canaanites. The twelve spies brought two different reports about their observations in Canaan. This implies that their perception of the land, people and the economy of the land had different interpretation of the reality. Which group was right?

In this democratic dispensation, there is a commonly adopted saying, "Majority must rule." The people who consent to this statement do not value the view of the minority even when they are right. What seems to be right in this situation is the majority view. In this case, 'what is right' is also subjective.

All twelve spies observed and spied the same land, people, and cities, etcetera. Ten of the twelve spies reported that the land was really good for occupation; but it required that they defeat the sons and giants of Anak. We should not dare take the land. The giants, sons of Anak are more powerful than we are. "We seemed like grasshoppers in our own eyes, and we looked the same to them." (Num 13:33) That was the report of the ten spies. Two of the twelve spies concurred with the rest that the land was good and was occupied by the giants, the sons of Anak. "We should go up and take possession of the land, for we can certainly do it" (Num 13:30). What was the difference between the two reports or two groups of spies who went to spy Canaan? The difference was the interpretation of reality.

The interaction of the ten spies with the giants, the sons of Anak brought fear in the perception of ten spies. The reality for these ten spies was to turn back to Egypt and give themselves as slaves to Egyptians. Two other spies perceived victory because of what God had promised them earlier on. Reality in human perspective was fear and failure to receive a promise from God. Reality in God's perspective was victory and possession of the land of promise.

Our perception of reality can either be positive or negative. The society can be perceived difficult and impossible for evangelism or receptive for the same. It all depends on how one interprets reality. As Christians and carriers of Christ's flag of victory our interpretation of reality is determined by our relationship and interaction with Jesus Christ, the Holy Spirit and the Scripture. The way a cross-cultural minister will interact with the society depends on how he interacts with Christ, the Holy Spirit and his Word. Christian reality is God. This reality is objective and absolute. Objective reality of a situation gives cross-cultural minister courage to pursue the truth and go for it. When we interact with our immediate society, the purpose is to develop relationships that can help us build bridges for effective communication into the respondent culture. Further, clear understanding of the reality may help the cross-cultural communicator to find solution to cultural, family and institutional conflicts that may exasperate the respondent society.

DISCUSSION QUESTIONS

- Discuss whether there is absolute reality.
- Define reality objectively.

6

Communication and the African Social Structure

- Introduction
- Definition of Cross-Cultural Communication
- Social Relationships and Communication in Africa
- The Effects of Social Structure on Cross-cultural Communication in Africa
- Discussion Questions

INTRODUCTION

MARGUERITE KRAFT NOTES, "DIFFERENCES in worldview present great difficulty in communication."[1] Generally, communication whether cross-culturally or not is not an easy business. Poor communication even in corporate world has always been a great challenge to successful business transaction. Preaching of the gospel is no exception in this challenge. Communication is the only means to successful accomplishment of the Great Commission to the ends of the earth and any social and community development endeavor.

The cross-cultural society is not a vacuum of worldview impact on gospel communication and the social development. The worldview assumptions of the cross-cultural missionary affect what the society believes, values and how people in that society relate with one another in respect of their statuses and roles. Therefore cross-cultural gospel communication and social development interventions should not be taken for granted in the African society.

---

1. Marguerite Kraft, *Understanding Spiritual Power: A Forgotten Dimension of Cross-Cultural Mission and Ministry*, 23.

This chapter will define cross-cultural communication; describe social relationships and communication, and the impact of social structure on cross-cultural communication of the gospel and social development interventions in the African society.

DEFINITION OF CROSS-CULTURAL COMMUNICATION

Though the world development agenda for the twenty-first century is globalization in a global village and culture, cross-cultural communication is still a challenge in corporate world, social development and missions. Therefore cross-cultural communication is not only a challenge in social development and corporate management; but missions too.

People from one part of the world are able to transact business with people from another part of the world whose cultural background is different. In the corporate business world, they talk about corporate culture and cross-cultural management; internationally and locally. In most cases, the communication principles applied in corporate business are both humanistic and biblical or spiritual.

Cross-cultural communication can simply be defined as relaying information to people whose cultural background and worldview are different from the communicator in culturally most effective way. Despite cultural differences, people in any society communicate with people they do not really know their worldviews, spiritually, culturally, economically, politically and socially. Communication in any given society always follows a certain pattern that easily disseminates what is encoded and decoded. African society; for example, has a way in which people get information without difficult. In Africa, this is possible because Africans depend on face to face talk with each other and have common assumptions for communication; although they have diverse cultures. Therefore, Christian communication in Africa takes the course of incarnation into the society's encoding and decoding systems that are culturally friendly and harnessed. In cross-cultural communication, what is desired is to get into a system of information dissemination that is effective, efficient and simple to the target ethnic group. Yet the basic way to communicate cross-culturally is learning and understanding the culture of the respondent society. *First*, the cultural differences between the encoder and decoder of the information being disseminated require critical study, analysis, evaluation and understanding. *Second*, learning how the decoder (respondent community) of the information interprets conventional symbols from a person considered stranger or foreigner is critical; hence requires use of the symbols primarily used by the decoder. *Third*, definition and choice of words in cross-cultural communication require a skill of incarnation into the respondent culture and language by the cross-cultural communicator. People define and use words according to their cultural context of reality. Words convey specific meanings professionally and culturally. Then, a cross-cultural communicator needs to understand the form and meaning of the words s/he wants to use in communication in the cross-cultural society. Cultural context of words should be maintained in cross-cultural communication. It is a principle in communication that communication should be as easy and simple as possible. All jargons should be avoided in communication with people who are laypersons to the particular profession. *Finally*, the cross-cultural communicator should always try his/her best to incarnate into the new culture rather than convincing or persuading the respondent society to incarnate into the missionary's culture.

The cross-cultural communicator's target is to communicate the gospel as precisely as possible, and as effectively as they can understand it without difficulties. This is why Incarnational ministry is a challenge and critical in missions and social development.

In cross-cultural communication, the message is more important than the messenger. The messenger should make sure that the message gets across to the decoder without any noise or interruptions. Paul Hiebert in *Perspectives* argues, "How can we communicate the gospel in other languages, and plant vital churches in cultures which differ markedly from our own?"[2] The answer to this argument is to learn how to communicate effectively in a cross-cultural society's language, symbols etcetera; African society in particular. The planted churches in Africa should be indigenous culturally, financially and the mode of worship.

SOCIAL RELATIONSHIPS
AND COMMUNICATION IN AFRICA

Social relationships can significantly affect the effectiveness of communication cross-culturally. In Africa, people relate to each other in various ways. The way the cross-cultural communicator relates to the natives can demonstrate and determine how effective the gospel can be relayed to

2. Hiebert, "Cultural Differences and the Communication of the Gospel", 377.

the African society. African societies have ethics and morals which are observed consciously or unconsciously to determine what is good or evil, righteousness or sin, moral or immoral. Ethics, values and morals are either specific to the particular society or universal. Therefore, they are subjective. Any cross-cultural communicator should first seek to understand the decoder's interest in the message. Considering the viewpoint of the African in the gospel is crucial in cross-cultural communication. Consequently basic understanding of what an African society calls sin, moral and ethical is significant. Morals, ethics and values that may be perceived incongruent to the Africans' perception may be noise to the gospel communication channels and social interventions in an African society. Feedback in communication in Africa may be got from personal interaction with the natives in an informal and or formal way.

The gospel preached in the power of the Holy Spirit will indeed convict people of sin. But it will depend on how sin is defined in that particular society. Studying what the African society considers to be sin can help the cross-cultural communicator to target his message toward behavioral and cultural change. In Africa, people of the same social class interact and communicate very often. In fact, it is easy to communicate with Africans who cooperate, relate and interact with you more often than any other. Hence, social relationships should be studied carefully in order to facilitate effective communication in a cross-cultural setting; whether for the gospel or social development interventions.

THE EFFECTS OF SOCIAL STRUCTURE
ON CROSS-CULTURAL COMMUNICATION IN AFRICA

The effects of social structure on cross-cultural communication can be devastating. In certain societies people communicate vertically while in others the communication is horizontal, and still in other societies it is both vertical and horizontal. Vertical communication style implies that the decision for the society is made by people in authority on top and it is communicated to the subjects down the line for implementation like in most political and caste systems.

The apostle Paul was conscious of this fact in Ephesus. In Ephesians 6:5–9, he addressed the issue of relationships between slaves and masters. The master-servant relationship in African society is detrimental to gospel communication unless done skillfully, the result may be exasperation.

The cross-cultural communicator ought to study how the members of the African society he reaches out with the gospel view their society leaders. For example, the *ngoni* chief in Malawi has authority over his subjects to the point that major decisions such as division of land for the society cannot be taken without his consent. Is s/he a master, boss or slave, servant leader? This will determine how effective the cross-cultural communicator can communicate the gospel to the *ngoni* society. As a cross-cultural communicator how do you view your audience: slaves, masters, or people of equal status with you? What is the African audience's view about you as a foreigner and gospel communicator in their society?

The church apart from being a religious and spiritual organization is also a social institution and an organism. In the church, people interact, relate, and relay information. They communicate either vertically or horizontally. They appoint and elect leaders for church government largely influenced by conceptualized reality in the African culture. Therefore, a cross-cultural communicator needs to study and understand the impact of social structure on communication.

The systems that are followed in electing public leaders to positions affect how people expect church leaders to be appointed or elected in African cultural setting. It also affects their perception of leaders whether they are masters, bosses or fellow servants in the Lord. However, the system of appointing or electing leaders in the church should be based on biblical principles and spiritual gifts. The cross-cultural church planter in Africa should study this worldview carefully in the society in which s/he is planting a church and ministering.

The growth of any local church in Africa depends on the church planter understanding the social structure and the culture of the African society and the church leadership put in place. A church planter and social development worker in Africa should make distinction between how people elect leaders publicly for public offices elsewhere and how the church needs to appoint or elect their leaders for the African church governance. For instance, if a church disciplines an offender in the church in most rural African society, all his or her relatives feel disciplined also. As a result, they stop attending the church services of that particular church because of a relative who is disciplined.

In public offices people elect the officers based on democratic processes. Most democratic systems are not recognizing the fruit of the Spirit and spiritual gifts of the people they elect into leadership. In public offices, people are elected because they have money to campaign and woo majority to vote for them. When they win they occupy and get the status of that office. For example, the person is voted into the office of the president not because of spiritual gifts or the fruit of the Spirit. There are several such offices within the state or outside. In contrast, the leadership in the church in Africa should consider spiritual gifts and biblical principles as basics for one to be considered for a church leadership position. Examples of biblical principles are salvation of the person, the manifestation of the fruit and gifts of the Holy Spirit in his/her life.

The social structure for the church ought to consider servant-leadership. Servant-leadership considers all society members as servants including the leader. Servant leaders sacrifice their statuses for the sake of the kingdom of God. They interact with every person at personal level while providing guidance to the church and people they interact with in the community. This is a big leadership challenge to most of Africans aspiring for church leadership because African model of leadership is master-servant type and communication is vertical in most cases.

Jesus Christ was a servant-leader (John 13:13–14). He never looked for positions in the Jewish society; yet he served wholeheartedly. He refused when they wanted to crown him king. He sacrificed his own blood for the society's welfare; although he was God. African society leaders look for praises, gifts and respect from their subjects while servant leaders sacrifice their lives for others. Status leadership is detrimental to church growth. However, the African leaders who led Africa to self independence in the early nineteen sixties, at least they sacrificed their lives without foreign support such as economic and political sanctions we see today.

The biblical base and principle for cross-cultural church growth is realization of the priesthood of all believers. Africans as a community people have strength in the priesthood of all believers. They think, work and decide as a community. The new society that is formed through conversion of indigenous African society members into Christianity should be taught the priesthood of all believers. Christian Schwarz observes, "The role of church leadership is to help its members to identify their gifts and to integrate them into appropriate ministries."[3] Church growth in Africa is not the responsibility of the cross-cultural minister

3. Schwarz, *Natural Church Development: A Guide to Eight Essential Qualities of Healthy Churches*, 24.

alone, but the natives too. The cross-cultural minister and the natives need to work corporately for church growth. In fact, the contribution of the natives to the church growth can be more effective than the efforts of the cross-cultural minister alone.

DISCUSSION QUESTIONS

- Define Cross-Cultural Communication.
- How can social relationship enhance cross-cultural communication in Africa?
- What is the role of the social structure in cross-cultural communication?

7

Missiological Application of Social-Cultural Anthropology in Africa

- Introduction
- The African Culture and Sin
- Cultural Concept of Sin
- Universal Concept of Sin
- The Role of the Bible and the Holy Spirit on Sin
- Discussion Questions

INTRODUCTION

SOCIAL-CULTURAL ANTHROPOLOGY IS AN effective tool for missiological and social development approach to the African society. Every society is culturally syncretic. It has an integration of beliefs from other cultures. Culture is a set of beliefs, values and worldviews that identifies a society.

In African culture, there are beliefs and values that are good and those that are evil or bad. It is also important to recognize that there is no culture that is holy, superior and good if it does not base its foundation on biblical principles, values and ethics.

Social-Cultural Anthropology and many other Social Sciences have contributed a lot to the success of missions; particularly in the twentieth and twenty-first centuries. Edward Rommen and Gary Corwin look at the relationship between social sciences and missiology to develop an understanding of the significance of studying social sciences in missions.[1] The church in Africa needs to be understood as an institution and a com-

---

1. Rommen and Corwin, "Missiology and the Social Sciences".

munity of believers existing in diverse cultures. As such, its purpose for missions will be directed consciously toward the right end. In this chapter, the author endeavors to discuss the cultural concept of sin and biblical role and perception of the same.

THE AFRICAN CULTURE AND SIN

The definition of sin can be subtle if taken for granted in an African culture. African societies are ethnocentric; as such, people think and behave in their cultural framework of reality. In African society there are virtues that are highly valued yet biblically they may be sinful, unethical and immoral. Most Africans in their society perform some cultural practices without critically and consciously looking at biblical basis of the same. Some of such practices are evil, though people practice them with clear conscience; for example, witchcraft, and polygamy, marriage by cohabitation, divination and so forth. In Africa, these cultural practices are done conscious free, yet they are biblically considered sinful. Still in some African countries, such as Swaziland, the king marries virgins almost every year. Traditionally, the practice is legitimate because it is morally considered right. It is done conscious free. So, the missionary needs to critically watch out such practices as these "for all have sinned and fallen short of the glory of God" (Rom 3:23).

Sin in Africa cannot be defined in the context of clear or unclear consciences of the particular people group or the society. The Spirit of God is more than our consciences in knowing, understanding and convicting sin. He can convict us even when our consciences are clear after performing a particular cultural practice. Our society in Africa may define certain cultural practices as good, right or evil. Nevertheless, the Bible sets the standards of right or wrong. This is Christian basis of the definition of sin, morals and ethics.

The role of the Holy Spirit in understanding what is evil or right in a cross-cultural society is really significant. The Holy Spirit was sent to give us godly understanding of right or wrong, good or evil and to distinguish between righteousness and wrongdoing. He leads us through the scriptures which teach us full counsel of God. Of course he uses our consciences but we cannot just trust our consciences to deal with the issues of sin; unless we are fully convinced by the scriptures. Sin is subtle. The second reason why the Holy Spirit came was to convict the world of guilt in regard to sin, righteousness and judgment (John 16:8). Sin cannot be defined accurately in cultural context rather than biblical. The Bible describes sin as lawlessness, falling short of God's glory and holiness, disobedience and etcetera. The Bible says, "Although they claimed to be wise, they became fools and exchanged the glory of the immortal God for images . . ." (Rom 1:22–23). The mind of mortal man without Christ is corrupt and desperately evil; it equates the immortal God with the works of his hands. Thus, it is important to study and understand the African perception and definition of sin.

CULTURAL CONCEPT OF SIN

"Man is not a sinner because he sins; he sins because he is a sinner."[2] By the sin of Adam, the whole human race became guilty of sin and corruption. Man is generally corrupt and evil; this is demonstrated in his actions against God, fellow man and environment.

The heart of unrepentant man is desperately evil and corrupt. The societies that have been formed by the corrupt people are likely to develop a culture that is contrary to godly or biblical principles. It does not matter whether the culture is considered good by the society practicing it or not. People have the tendency of lowering godly standards because they are corrupt, subtle and evil. Hence cultural definition of sin should not be taken for granted in Africa and cannot be genuine.

Most African traditional celebrations include beer drinking, ritualistic dancing either to the ancestral spirits or deities and some of these activities are accredited to the idols. These activities are significant to the African society's identity and cultural practices. African culture is preserved through such rituals as initiations, drinking parties, traditional religious worship, traditional music and dances. In most, if not all African societies sin does not include the behavior of drinking beer or getting drunk with beer, multiple marriage partners, African traditional initiations and traditional dances as sins.

If the cross-cultural minister talks about the evils of these activities as performed by local society members, the message is considered confrontational to their culture and the belief and value systems. As a result, people may reject both the message and the messenger. Particularly Western missionaries have logic which is not conceptualized by a tradi-

2. Adams, *A Theology of Christian Counseling*, 142.

tional African. So, when the gospel is presented logically to confront these practices, the reception may sometimes be negative and frustrating to the cross-cultural minister. According to the society, these activities may not be considered as sins. Culturally, sin may be defined as any activities of disobedience to cultural leadership, rules and principles of the society that have been accepted as morally and ethically right. This definition is inferior to biblical concept and meaning of sin. Thus, care should be exercised by cross-cultural gospel communicators in a foreign culture.

The second view is the issue of deity. Due to corruption of human heart, the definition of deity is generic. Some African societies venerate things or created beings rather than God, the creator of the universe and humanity. This view also affects how people define sin. Is idol worship sin? Certainly in Africa, this will depend on whether you argue from Christian or African cultural perspective.

Therefore, a cross-cultural minister needs to study and understand the African society's culture in order to address issues of sin and deity adequately. It is important to recognize that sin cannot easily be defined in cultural context. It further depends on what the society considers evil, right, and good, wrong, bad and god. A cross-cultural minister should not assume that sin means the same to every people unless universal and biblical concept of sin is established in that particular society or religion.

UNIVERSAL CONCEPT OF SIN

In every society there are practices which are generally considered sinful. For example, covetousness, murder, sexual affairs with somebody's wife or husband, fighting; these and many others are universally accepted as sins. Issues like idolatry, gossips, cohabitation and sexual relationships with unmarried women or girls may not be considered as sins in some African societies. Yet, it is important that a cross-cultural minister studies the trends of behavior and attitude of the African society when ministering cross-culturally in order to understand the definition of sin contextually.

The concept of having deity in a society lays down a premise for dealing with the issue of sin in an African society. The cross-cultural minister ought to study the African society's view of a deity before introducing the supreme deity, the Lord of lords, Jehovah God. However, care needs to be taken because every society considers their deity as Supreme Being also. The supreme being of every society culturally demands respect, honour and worship. And these activities are carried on even when the people are converted into another religion-even Christianity. So, when they worship even idols, they feel they are doing a duty to their God. Unless people in the African society have the concept of God of all nations, the creator of heavens and earth and all what is in them, their zeal for worship and the concept or definition of sin is subtle and makes them idolaters.

The righteousness of God who is Jesus Christ (2 Cor 5:21) is the standard to judge whether what people practice is sin or not. If what people do is contrary to the standards set by Jesus Christ in his earthly life and the scriptures, then, those practices are just rituals and evil.

THE ROLE OF THE BIBLE AND THE HOLY SPIRIT ON SIN

Since it is deceptive to trust human consciences in defining sin culturally, then, the role of the Bible and the Holy Spirit is critically significant to consider. The role of the Bible and the Holy Spirit in understanding and defining sin should never be compromised in any way; particularly in Africa. Sin is subtle. The mind of an African as well as any other people in the world is incapacitated to discern subtlety of sin since Adam's fall. Romans 1:18–32, clearly reveals the state of man's heart. Humanity is corrupt and evil. If this is how corrupt the mind of man is, how then, can his conscience be trusted when s/he practices what s/he desires?

In the same epistle to the church at Rome, Apostle Paul said, "For all have sinned and fall short of the glory of God" (Rom 3:23). The condition of human heart since the fall cannot be trusted for godliness, righteousness and honour of God. It is subject to error; unless transformed by the power of God through repentance and new birth. Therefore, the society to which a cross-cultural minister is called is as corrupt as their hearts are revealed in the scriptures and the practices of their culture. Culture is the product of the society's perception of reality before and after the fall. The perception of reality with the condition of the human heart as described in Romans chapter 1 threatens the trust of human consciences in defining sin culturally; whether in Africa or elsewhere in the world.

The Holy Spirit knows man from inside out. He knows the condition of the heart from which comes the knowledge about God and everything else. This is one of the reasons why a cross-cultural minister needs to allow and depend on the Holy Spirit to convict and transform lives of the members of the society without being prejudiced with his own cultural imperfections and biases. The society should not be judged in the lenses of the culture of the cross-cultural minister. No matter how perfect our culture may be perceived, it has been tainted with imperfections of our hearts inherited from the fall of humanity in Adam (Rom 5:18–19). Our culture without repentant hearts, renewed minds and justified personalities cannot judge what is right or wrong in any culture accurately. So, when we come to Jesus Christ with our imperfections He is righteous and just to forgive us our sins and justify us from the imperfections (1 John 1:9). It is until then that we can see clearly what is right or wrong in our culture or another culture. A cross-cultural minister should not judge the culture of the society where he is a minister as evil or right in the light of his/her culture. The judgment should be in the light of the scriptures and the leading of the Holy Spirit.

DISCUSSION QUESTIONS

- How would you define sin in African cultural concept?
- What would save you as framework for the definition of sin?
- Discuss the role of the Bible and the Holy Spirit in the definition of sin.

8

The Missionary and African Culture Change

- Introduction
- Reasons for Culture Change in Africa
- The Role of a Missionary in Culture Change in Africa
- Challenges to Culture Change in Africa
- Facilitators of Culture Change in Africa
- Managing the Results of Culture Change in Africa
- Discussion Questions

INTRODUCTION

SINCE CULTURE IS DYNAMIC, change is inevitable. Yet culture change is not easy as some people may suppose. There are several factors to consider in implementing culture change in Africa; and anywhere else in the world. *First*, we need to consider the reason for the culture change. Why should this culture, change? *Second*, the role of the facilitators of culture change in the society that needs change. What should facilitators of culture change do to have it changed? *Third*, the roadblocks to culture change and organization of the African society we target to institute culture change. *Fourth*, what should change in that culture? *Finally*, having the culture changed is one thing and managing the results of culture change is another.

The target of the gospel is to change the depraved heart of a sinner and make that person a child of God. Since the fall of humanity through Adam people are lost and misdirected by the devil. The depraved mind of mankind in Africa and anywhere in the world has developed value, belief systems and cultures that are detrimental to appreciating God's love and his redemptive plan through Jesus Christ. The relationship of man with God is alienated and needs a Savior and reconciliation. The mediator or arbitrator of this reconciliation is the man, Jesus Christ (1 Tim.2:5). Therefore, African and any other culture which is the product of depraved mind, value and belief systems of the societies certainly need change. It is imperative also to note that God is the initiator of this culture change. As such, the role of the Holy Spirit in culture change is crucial.

REASONS FOR CULTURE CHANGE IN AFRICA

Culture change takes both rationalism and the work of the Holy Spirit in the respondent African society. Unless the gospel makes sense in the African society, culture change may remain a great challenge to missionary work and social development. Both western missionaries and the respondent society have biases on their concept of reality and rationale. The difference between the missionary and the respondent society is the perception of reality and rationalization of facts and theories of the culture that needs change because both the facilitator and the respondent society have cultural biases.

At this point let me remind you what is discussed in the previous chapter. No culture is holy, superior, inferior, good or evil by itself. Culture can be perceived as good or bad only when it has been screened through the scriptures, biblical principles and the work of the Holy Spirit. But, why do we need culture change in Africa?

First, because the people who develop the cultures of our African societies are basically evil (Rom 1:18–32; 3:23; 12:1–2) and they need change from their hearts and mind. No matter how good our culture may seem to be, it is the product of a depraved mind. The humanistic reality is alien to God's reality. Hence, culture change in Africa is necessary.

Second, African culture and worldview formation include beliefs, values, rituals and practices that are detrimental to God's perception of his people. God is the absolute reality of humankind. In fact, actualization of man's image is depended on accepting God's terms of lifestyle. Therefore, people in Africa cannot understand this reality unless their perception is significantly changed through preaching of the word. Africans need personal relationship with God to have their culture changed.

Third, culture in African societies may hinder character change in the people who practice it. Culture can be deceptive because the whole society interprets its reality in terms of their worldview; and therefore consider it right. If in their perception, God is transcendent and not immanent, their interpretation may be that he exists remotely and does not care; they may end up venerating created beings as God because they can access them easily and is relevant to their daily life. God's reality is absolute and immutable.

Fourth, culture is ethnocentric and generational. Yet the gospel is universal and transgenerational. God does not only care about one ethnic group or one generation of people over the other. He is God of all nations and generations; his plan is to reconcile all nations from every society despite their historical, social, economical, political and religious backgrounds through Jesus Christ.

Fifth, the theological views about Christ in some traditional religions are subtle and heretic. In some African societies, religion and culture are but one thing. For example, in Muslim dominated societies in Africa Islam and culture is one. Religion sets the rituals, beliefs, values and worldview of the society. The people who practice this culture in such societies have wrong concepts about the gospel and Christ. Hence culture change in Africa is necessary.

In Hindu religion, Christ is just as one of their gods. Their culture is conceptualized in the practices of their traditional religion. As such, culture change need to be instituted in such societies. Some countries in Africa have Hindu religion and society. For example in Malawi, there is a Hindu society.

Sixth, failure of people to develop significantly in social, spiritual, political and economic life may call for culture change in the society. The culture change may provide a way to syncretize philosophies and methods of social and economic development of the society. This is important because people learn from others about what and how they do things that enhance productivity of life in the society.

THE ROLE OF A MISSIONARY
IN CULTURE CHANGE IN AFRICA

1. To study the basic African fundamental principles of the culture that needs change. This can orient the missionary to the social structures, values, beliefs, and rituals of the African society that need change. He will also be able to perceive things from the African's point of view. In doing this, the missionary will be draining out his cultural biases and assumptions he might have conceptualized and help people change their behaviors through preaching of the gospel of repentance and socio-economic interventions.

2. *To be the catalyst for culture change in Africa.* Involve members of the targeted society in culture change in Africa. Discuss with members of the African society the weaknesses and strength of their culture towards their faith in God and social development of their society. The process of culture change in Africa should not be implemented until there is evidence that members of the African society have understood the reason for change. Let them suggest the course of action to be taken for the way forward.

3. *To expose the African society to new information and experiences about spiritual, social and community development.* He can do this by preaching and teaching the truth about God from the scriptures. Charles Kraft notes, "It is at the level of worldview that the cross-cultural Christian witness seeks to bring change as a result of the entrance of the gospel of Jesus Christ."[1] When the gospel makes sense in the spiritual and social lives of people in the African society, change of culture is expected inevitably. Certainly, this calls the cross-cultural communicator to contextualize the message so that it becomes relevant to real life situation and challenges.

4. *To pray for culture change in Africa.* The intervention of the Holy Spirit in culture change in Africa is crucial and desirable. It is God's will that people change their evil cultural beliefs and practices. Therefore a cross-cultural missionary ought to consult God through fervent prayers for the change of culture in Africa. The African culture cannot change unless there is change in worldview. Worldview change influences thinking patterns that eventually change culture and peoples' behavior and action.

5. *To plant churches and start social development interventions.* A church is an agent of culture change.[2] The church is the body of Christ existing to be a witness for Christ in the society. In fact, the church founded on the faith in Jesus Christ demonstrates the love of God and eventually brings about a desired culture change in Africa and any other society. The ultimate change the church and social interventions can bring in the African society is a behavioral and perceptual change

1. Charles Kraft, *Anthropology for Christian Witness*, 436.
2. Kietzman and Smalley, "The Missionary's Role in Culture Change", 481.

through the preaching of the gospel for repentance. The church must be the light to the society in Africa. The social development work in Africa should demonstrate the caring love of Jesus Christ for the needy community. In fact, people change through observation of a way of life of the missionary and the social development worker in relation to how s/he lives with the indigenous in the society.

The church must continue to be the light to the world. People must be able to see the character of Jesus Christ in the life of the cross-cultural missionary.

CHALLENGES TO CULTURE CHANGE IN AFRICA

Culture change though desirable, it is not easily implemented in any society. There are many problems challenging its change. However, the following are major challenges of culture change in Africa.

1. *Worldview change.* "Worldview tends to conserve old ways and are resistant to change."[3] Worldview is the total sum of beliefs, values and rituals of the African society. Culture is the product of the African worldview because it interprets its perception of reality. Therefore, to implement culture and worldview change in Africa is not as easy. "Worldview change is possible; but it takes time, exposition of new information and new experiences."[4] The missionary or cross-cultural development worker should carefully study the African society's worldview and then implement changes by preaching and living the gospel.

2. *African Social Structures.* Every society is socially, economically, politically and spiritually organized and structured. An African society is not an exception. An African society is communal and oral. As such, decision for a change would certainly involve the entire society understanding the need for a change. As an oral society, communicating the reasons for culture change in Africa may take quite some time because Africans are generally not a reading and time conscious society. Further, culture change in Africa may threaten certain royalties. Once such threats are identified, the change may likely be objected.

Jesus Christ was born a revolutionary leader and King. When King Herod heard of his birth he was shaken and geared to destroy Christ the

3. Charles Kraft, *Anthropology for Christian Witness*, 22.
4. Ibid, 22.

Lord. The reason for the plan of this destruction was that his position was threatened. Yet Jesus Christ was not born to overthrow the Roman Empire of which Herod was the King. Jesus Christ wanted change of the peoples' perception of God and His Kingdom. The change that Jesus Christ brought was resisted throughout Jesus' life time. Yet not all people resisted it. Some people even among the Jews believed in Jesus Christ and they were saved. God is not the executor of penalties; but the giver of love and sacrifice for the sins of the world.

Some societies elsewhere in the world are organized into castes and other social classes. The castes and the social classes are threats to culture change. In caste societies the classes of people are absolutes of the society. These and many other institutions are not easily moved toward culture change unless there is change in their worldview and the thinking patterns which may be influenced by repentance and social change in the society.

3. Religion. People in every society have a religion and venerate their deity as a duty they owe him/her. In Africa, most people have traditional religions which influence their worldviews and thinking patterns. If anyone brings a religion that is perceived as foreign or new, people become sensitive and resist the changes. It seems natural for people to resist change of any kind. The Supreme Being or deity is very difficult to change when implementing culture change in Africa and anywhere else. Since their worldview has taught them that their deity is supreme, good and cares for the society's needs, cultural change is difficult in most African societies. Therefore a cross-cultural missionary needs to study and understand the religion of the society where s/he serves as a facilitator for culture change in Africa.

4. Language and Communication. Africans are proud of their local languages. As oral society, Africans communicate well in their local languages more than in any other language. The western missionary and the social development worker need to learn the local language of the African community for effective culture change. As oral and a communal society, Africans' decision is in most cases a consultative process and a 'majority must rule' concept. Whatever, the community has decided whether for culture change or not, it is final and every member of the society must be subjected to it.

Further, African society has respect for elders. However, in the contemporary African society young people are also exerting pressure for change of the old traditions of elderly mentality. They are also the majority of the population. Therefore, communication for culture change in Africa must target the both the elders and young generation of the society; otherwise change may not be possible.

FACILITATORS OF CULTURE CHANGE IN AFRICA

Culture change in Africa can best be facilitated by the following:

1. Opinion Leaders. Though it is hard to identify opinion leaders in the African society, yet they are desirable for culture change. Church history has taught us about Emperor Constantine of the Roman Empire that he espoused Christianity and declared it a Christian Empire. His three sons who succeeded him successively took their father's view about Christian faith more seriously than their father.[5] But there is one danger with this; nominal Christianity may result out of it. Emperor Constantine was a nominal Christian himself.

Fredrick Chiluba of Zambia in 1992 when he was elected president of the republic of Zambia, declared Zambia as a Christian nation on the day he was sworn in office as the republican president. But not every Zambian is a Christian to date; and Chiluba himself is answering corruption charges in the Zambian High court.[6] The American currency, a dollar, has an inscription "In God we trust." Until now not every American trusts God even for a daily bread. Nevertheless, opinion leaders can help transform the societies culturally; though such transformation is repugnant in Christianity. Opinion leaders make quick social and spiritual changes in the mindset of the society. They are desirable in Africa for culture changes.

2. Ability to incarnate into the African culture. The cross-cultural missionary and the social development worker should incarnate into the African culture if they want to institute culture change. The process of incarnation will help the cross-cultural missionary and the social worker learns the skills of communication that are effective in a particular African society. Then, he will communicate with the natives with minimum linguistic and cultural barriers. In addition, s/he will understand why people in that society think and behave the way they do. Incarnation further help change the culture of people when the mis-

5. Latourette, *A History of Christianity*, 93.
6. Post Newspaper, April 2009.

sionary and the social worker provide new information that is relevant to peoples' spiritual and social needs and lifestyle.

3. *Identify Social needs that can act as communication bridges into the Society's Culture.* Facilitators of culture change in Africa should deliberately engage themselves into providing social facilities that most people in Africa need. People of any society can easily learn the love of God through social interventions. Patrick Dixon observes, "People should feel the love of Jesus Christ not only in words; but in its practical sharing of it."[7] Africans respond quickly to social interventions in their communities; thus, facilitating culture change much faster than otherwise anticipated.

4. *Ability to discern the guidance of the Holy Spirit.* The Holy Spirit is the key facilitator of culture change in any society. Africans, though difficult they may be, the Holy Spirit can help bring culture change without broken relationships in the society. Therefore, the cross-cultural missionary and the social worker should obey and discern the direction the Holy Spirit is leading the process of culture change in Africa. In fact, the work of transforming cultures, behaviors of the proponents of particular cultural views and belief and value systems is for the Holy Spirit in collaboration with the cross-cultural missionary and the social worker.

MANAGING THE RESULTS
OF CULTURE CHANGE IN AFRICA

History teaches that the whole of North Africa embraced Christianity as early as the first century. The Bible has recordings of the countries of North Africa such as Egypt, Ethiopia, Sudan and so forth. Why is it that most of these countries are now typical Muslim countries? What was the problem with Christianity? Was nominal Christianity, the problem?

In this book, we have learnt that culture is dynamic. And as such, if not well managed the culture change may just be a social veil that may be put on and off by the adherent of the culture in Africa. The African societies that may change their culture can eventually revert to the old life style and culture and never notice any significance of the change of the same as time passes by.

Culture change in Africa can best be managed by the following institutions:

7. Dixon, *Out of the Ghetto and Into the City: A Radical Call to Social Action*, 24–25.

1. The Church. The church is an agent of culture change just as we have observed in this book. The Church is a community of converted, repented and spirit-filled people. According to Jesus Christ (Acts 1:8), the church is the community of witnesses who have received the power and are filled with the Holy Spirit to preach the gospel to people of all tribes. The presence of the church in the African community can continue impacting that society for Christ as long as that church obeys the commands of the Lord Jesus Christ. Keep the fires burning! The culture change in Africa may be permanent if the church keeps on discipling the converts and providing counseling and guidance to the society.

2. Spirit-filled Leadership. After the society has changed its culture as a result of the influence of the gospel and social interventions, the church needs to have spirit-filled leadership to develop and maintain culture change in Africa. African societies shall always have their culture changed either for good or for bad. Culture is dynamic. There are many institutions and factors to influence culture change in Africa; and Christianity is just one of such institutions.

3. Social Development Interventions. The church in Africa actively participates in social and spiritual development for the sake of society benefit. The gospel approach to the African society should be holistic; such that social and spiritual needs must be met right in the church. This also means that theological or ministerial training should be designed to train pastors even in the development work of the society.

In any society, people change the culture when something challenging the present view makes sense. They adapt it into their culture. In other words there is syncretism in the most African cultures; just as it is in any other culture. Spirit-filled leadership of the church can manage and guide the culture change in Africa better.

DISCUSSION QUESTIONS

- Why is it important to consider organization of the society when desiring culture change?
- Discuss the role of opinion leaders in culture change.
- What can sustain the results of culture change?

9

The Church

- Introduction
- The Church as a Community
- The Church as an Institution
- Discussion Questions

INTRODUCTION

THE STUDY OF SOCIAL-CULTURAL Anthropology as an academic pursuit can be of no value if not linked to the purpose of the Church for the society. Jesus Christ founded the church in the culture of Jewish people. When he commissioned his disciples to be his witnesses to the ends of the earth, he was very aware that the gospel will encounter cultures of the people living there. Therefore it is imperative that as we study Social-Cultural Anthropology, we should turn to the Church as a community and institution with its unique culture, beliefs and values.

Basically, the church was born among the people of a culture in Israel. Jewish culture was the primary culture in which the father and founder of a church, Jesus Christ, was born, grew up and birthed the church. In fact, Jesus Christ himself understood what it meant to live and minister to people with a culture. He formed a distinguished community out of the Jewish community and culture and developed relationships with people of a culture.

Now it is assumed that you have some glimpses of the Cross-Cultural Ministry, social development and what it takes to be with people of a different culture. The missionary should found the community of believers in any society.

THE CHURCH AS A COMMUNITY

The word church has evolved from its original state *ecclesia* to mean the summoned assembly, to a building and denomination in the twentieth and twenty-first centuries. It is important to ask what a person means when the word church is mentioned. It means many things to many people depending on their subject of discussion. Patrick Ryan defines the church as people of God.[1] It also means a body of Christ – body of believers; yet to some it just means a house of prayer and still to others it means a denomination. While all these meanings are accepted, it is important for the sake of this discussion to recognize the church as a body of Christ, also translated the community of believers as asserted by the apostle Paul in the epistle to the Corinthian church (1 Cor 12:14, 27).

The church as a body of believers is a community with unique beliefs, values, rituals and a culture. *First*, the church was founded by Jesus Christ in the Jewish community. The Jewish community had a culture based on the values and beliefs inherited from their patriarchs; Abraham, Isaac and Jacob. It is also important to understand at this point that these patriarchs were not Jews and were not a community by themselves.

A Jewish community was born out of the sons of Jacob and the generation that followed in the country of their slavery-Egypt. In that community, people cherished and practiced their culture in the worship of God. Some have erred by thinking that Jewish culture is Christian culture, therefore, it must be embraced. There were evil practices in that culture also which did not please God and Jesus rebuked the Pharisees and Sadducees for practicing such without paying attention to the teachings of the scriptures (Matt 5:16; 15:1–9). *Second*, when Jesus Christ was born in the Jewish community, he immediately became and by birth a member of Jewish community. He grew up obeying and observing the Jewish culture (Luke 2:21–24, 41–52). It is important to note that Jesus Christ observed the culture in which he grew up without breaking the law of God. It is possible that people took Jesus Christ for granted because he was just like any Jew in the Jewish society. Yet, his obedience to the Jewish law and culture gave him milliard opportunities to minister to his immediate audience effectively. *Third*, Jesus Christ was a bona fide member of the Jewish community; he met the requirements of that society through incarnation. He was circumcised on the eighth day as it was required in

1. Ryan, "Building a New Idea and Image of the Church", 9.

the Jewish Law. He observed Sabbath as required by God not the Jewish culture. The Jews observed Sabbath ritually not godly. Therefore, he knew, understood and observed the Jewish culture without doubt. When he founded the church in that culture amongst people who also were indoctrinated in the same culture, he knew what it means to minister among the cultured people.

Certainly, Jesus Christ was against some beliefs, rituals and values that his immediate community observed about God and the gospel. In some circumstances he rebuked the Jews about ritualistic observation of the laws of Moses, for not recognizing the fulfillment of some prophetic events in him (Matt 5:17), limiting God's love for all nations to Jewish community only and etcetera. He, however, recommended some cultural practices in the Jewish community such as tithing (Matt 23:23–24), and temple worship on Sabbath days. In fact, he observed Sabbath himself even more than ritualistic observation of the same by the Jews (John 9:13–15). Therefore, the church was born out of a community with a culture. The Jews were more patriotic to their culture than to God. Then, they observed their rituals more strictly than God's commands. Sometimes people become patriotic to their cultural practices more than to God their creator. The cross-cultural minister and the social worker, therefore, should understand these concepts and provide a linkage for gospel or social development communication to the society.

The church is a community with distinctive beliefs, rituals, values, and a culture. A church as a body of believers is a community of people who believe in Jesus Christ. Generally, the church community is distinguished from other communities because of the faith its members have in Jesus Christ as the Lord and Saviour of those who believe in his name. They also value the Bible as the inspired Word of God and that life on earth is but short stay. Members of the church community fellowship together and share their spiritual, economic, political and social needs (Acts 2:42; 4:32–35; 6:1–9). Church fellowship must be transcultural, multi-racial and multi-linguistic. It must be realized that members of the church are people from different cultural, social, economic, linguistic, political and religious background. Hence, when ministering to such a community, care must be taken to avoid racial, emotional, political, social and spiritual casualties.

The administration of the Holy Communion in the church signifies what community the church is. These and many other beliefs, rituals and values distinguish this community from any other communities in

the world. Like any other community, members of the church community share the same beliefs, values, rituals and culture. The culture of the
church community is based on the biblical principles of love, humility,
unity and Christian values. Thus, it is important to recognize the church
as a community with a culture.

The church is a community in the world but not of the world. Like I
said, in the previous discussions about the society, the society or a community is identified by its culture, belief systems and core values. David
Hesselgrave says that the church community is identified by a supraculture.[2] Members of this community must voluntarily join it upon making
a confession of faith that Jesus Christ is their Lord and Savior. Members
of church community are not identified by cards of membership as it
is the case in some countries that citizens are identified by registration
cards. In some countries membership is by birth, residence or registration. It is not so with church community membership. A person can have
a membership card of his/her denomination; but a member of a *catholic*
church must be born again to acquire membership for church community, a body of Christ. After the confession of Jesus Christ as Lord and
Savior, the member should believe s/he is saved and is a member of the
church community. We have learnt that members of a particular society
give allegiance to the leadership and observe beliefs, rituals and values
of that particular society. In a church community, members are required
no less than the same to their God. Jesus is the Chief Shepherd (John
10:11; 1 Peter 5:4) and head (leader) of the body of believers (1 Cor.
11:3; 12:12–13) (church community). It is this community that Jesus
Christ is the Savior not only for Jews but for all nations on earth. He
commissioned believers to be his witnesses to the ends of the earth.

THE CHURCH AS AN INSTITUTION

The church is not only a community but an institution also. What makes a
church an institution? Well, such inquiry mind is appreciated in discover-
ing the truth about the God of the nations.

A church is an institution because it has some rules that govern it
and give it a purpose and direction. Like we have learnt above, the church
community has leaders, beliefs, values and a culture. A church as an or-

---

2. Hesselgrave, *Communicationg Christ Cross-Culturally: An Introduction to
Missionary Communication*, 305.

ganization or institution also has leaders, beliefs, values and culture. The culture of the church is conceptualized in the worldview of God as the absolute reality. Therefore, members of the church institution must by all means conform to the standards that are biblical, spiritual and holy according to the Scriptures. They must cultivate the characteristics worthy a Christian. The Bible defines morals and ethics of Christians who are members of the church in the context of understanding their culture.

God expects the church as an institution to demonstrate the characteristics that are no less than those Jesus Christ himself gave in the Jewish community and culture. Though he was in the very nature God, he humbled himself to the level of a servant (John 13:13–14; Phil 2:5–8). Members of the church must demonstrate no less than these characteristics in their execution of duty to one another.

The governing rules of a church as an institution should at all cost avoid being secular in standards. The church as an institution is a heavenly body on earth, to give light to the world that is in darkness. Hence, no lower standards are expected, as long as it continues to represent Jesus Christ on earth as the light in the darkness.

The church is like a family institution where members find solace, fellowship and communion for worship. In Africa, the family is extended to generations and relationships from both maternal and paternal lineage. It is for this reason that communalism is highly valued in African societies. Members of the church as an institution interact with each other while observing biblical morals and ethics and commune together in the sharing of the Holy Communion.

DISCUSSION QUESTIONS

- Define the church as a community of believers.
- Discuss the purpose of the church as a community of believers and as an institution.

10

Christian Leadership Development:
An African Culture in Perspective

- Introduction
- African Cultural Leadership Models: Lessons
  for Post-democratic Church Leadership Aspirants
- Organization of the African Society
- Democratic African Leadership Model (DALM)
- Biblical Model of Electing Church Leadership
- Affirming the Role of the Holy Spirit in Developing
  Emerging Church Leaders
- Biblical Images of Leadership for Church Leaders
  in African Context.
- Basic Elements of Leadership in Africa
- The How of African Leadership
- Importance of Leadership in the Church and Society
- Typical Christian Leadership Images
- Evaluating the Call of African Christian Leaders
  into Ministry
- Conclusions
- Discussion Questions

INTRODUCTION

THIS STUDY ARGUES THAT Christian leadership is an asset and a unique
calling to the church ministries in Africa. And that the church exists
in an environment where culture is invaluably considered a determinant

element for leadership development, people's thinking patterns and behaviour of the society. Hence, the study of the impact of the African culture in relation to Christian leadership development in Africa is essential. The growth of the church or any organization basically depends on the development of leadership and how that leadership handles people in respect of their personal and professional goals, culture, beliefs, and values. Christian leadership needs to evaluate and consider the importance of the spiritual gifts and the culture of people in the church as a Christian organization with its goals of developing other leaders. Culture is inherently considered a valuable asset for social development of the society. Whenever the church is planted or a social work starts in a society, raising the culturally fitting Christian leadership is a challenge. However, this study argues that Christian leaders who have a vision, goal and purpose can influence and develop the potential in others, despite African cultural diversity. In this chapter, the author will evaluate the historical leadership development models in Africa, and critically examine the impact of African political culture on Christian leadership development, particularly of the twenty-first century Christian organization.

Understanding Christian leadership development in African cultural perspective is foundational and significant for church growth and social development of the African society. The church is primarily called to proclaim the gospel to all creation (Mark 16:15), yet the means to that effect requires a critical study of spiritual and socio-cultural leadership of the community in which the church exists in order to overcome barriers of communication for church growth and social development. How the Christian leadership can be the agent for change spiritually, economically, socially and culturally in meeting the needs of the community is just as important. The church is both a spiritual and social institution of the society. People interact, communicate and find solace in the church. In fact, the church under its Christian leadership is expected to provide an environment of interaction with people of all walks in the society.

Cultural challenges are crucial to Christian leadership development in any society. Most church planters perceive people as souls and not as humans; while social development workers perceive people as humans. The dichotomy between the two is devastating to the society's success spiritually and socially. With such an understanding, cultural structures that form the worldview of the society are disrespected and taken for granted. The result of such a view is perpetual preaching of the gospel that people do not see relevance to every day needs and the need for salvation. People have spiritual, physical, and social needs. Hence, the church needs to develop leaders who can integrate and appreciate all peoples' needs and seize the opportunity for church growth through holistic ministry.

Man is body, soul and spirit; and should be understood as such. Christian leadership is culturally trained to build the holistic leadership capacity for church growth in the geographical area where they minister. If leaders cannot be trained to fit the African cultural needs of the church, and the society the result may be stunted church growth and exasperation. "Jesus Christ treated people as persons."[1] Christian leaders anticipating growth looks at people as lost human beings as well as lost souls. People always look for a leader in their society who can lead them to the solution of their long standing spiritual, social, political or economic problems. If that is the plea of the society, then, how much more the church will need spiritually and culturally fitting Christian leaders? It is important to understand and mitigate the spiritual, social and physical needs of the society through church ministries. To do this successfully, Christian leadership development is critical. The African church needs to develop Christian leaders who can integrate spiritual, social and physical needs of the African society. The gospel should be relevant to peoples' needs whether spiritual, social or economic. God cares for the whole person not just a soul. This is why he provides resources for salvation, deliverance, healing, food and money to prosper the society.

Every society has its own cultural leadership challenges. Africa has its own leadership challenges ranging from political, social to spiritual and economical. As Jo-Ansie van Wyk observes that the perception is that African leaders failed to lead the African states to sustainable development by its leaders' admission, in crisis due to its loss of the spirit of its traditional leadership and postcolonial "questionable leadership."[2] Africa as a society has its own spiritual and socio-economic challenges that require traditional leadership that understands the African situation and context of issues affecting the continent not only theoretically but practically as well and address them accordingly. There is political and spiritual leadership crisis in Africa. The largest population of

1. Dempster et al., *Called & Empowered: Global Missions in Pentecostal Perspectives*, 312.

2. Van Wyk, "Political Leaders in Africa: Presidents, Patrons or Profiteers?" 4.

African is either refugees, or economic asylum seekers within or outside Africa which probably has caused brain drain, African Diaspora and of late xenophobia. The major cause of these social problems in Africa is leadership. As the president of Uganda, Yoweli Museveni admits that Africa's problem is leadership.[3] However, it is also important to realize that Africa as a continent faces great economic and social challenges that the issue of brain drain should be understood as economic survival for the Africans who have skills to sell not only in Africa, but to the larger world labour market. The issue of brain drain is such a difficult thing to be sorted out by one continent or country because it also involves labour market influx worldwide.

Christian leadership of church growth and social development in Africa ought to understand these challenges as they plan for church growth or social development work in Africa. ". . . Change is now so rapid that past experience is no longer sufficient to help us plan for the future as leaders. We need to know the best we can where the world is headed."[4] Political or religious leaders in Africa must understand that any mistake they make in their leadership in their generation will have an impact on the next generation and can lead the society into spiritual and socio-economic disrepute. In Christian leadership development the incumbent leaders should provide an environment and models for growth in the potentially emerging leaders. It should also be appreciated that cultural leadership style does not necessarily elect situational leaders unless the whole community sees its importance. Traditionally, in a monarchical leadership system and cultural setting, leaders are elected through family lineage, purpose, age and popularity. That is how caste system also works in India. Potentially inspired, emerging Christian and political leaders who do not have any linkage to the royal or the caste may not be considered for leadership development. With this background, it is imperative to affirm the role of the Holy Spirit in emerging African Christian and political leaders.

3. Museveni, *What is Africa's problem? Speeches and writings on Africa*, 2.

4. Dempster et al., *Called & Empowered: Global Missions in Pentecostal Perspectives*, 253.

AFRICAN CULTURAL LEADERSHIP MODELS: LESSONS FOR POST-DEMOCRATIC CHRISTIAN LEADERSHIP ASPIRANTS

The post-democratic Christian leaders must carefully learn from the history of the continent's political leadership models if the continent will achieve spiritual, political, social, peace and economic viability of Africa. Edgar Elliston notes that church leadership is often impacted by secular leadership.[5] Africa like many other continents was basically governed by monarchical system of leadership. And there are a few other monarchies in existence in Africa; such as, Swaziland and Lesotho in Southern Africa and Morocco in North Africa. Kings and Chiefs ruled Africa until when Africa was colonized in the eighteenth and nineteenth centuries when monarchical system of governance was replaced by colonial political leadership system. As Christian leaders who develop future leaders what lessons do we draw from such cultural practices?

Slave trade worked alongside the monarchical system of governance before Africa was colonized. Slavery was successful in Africa because Africans were organized in families, tribes, clans and kingdoms led by kings and or chiefs. Africans are tribal and oral societies. It just required the slave masters to consult with the king or chief, and the chief would sell the strongest people of his/her kingdom whom he considered to be his threats. This means that chiefs and kings did not have means of developing the potential emerging leaders of their kingdoms. Some of the people who were perceived to be trouble makers were actually intellectuals and potential future leaders of the society. Second, leadership was perceived to be family inheritance or leaders were born. No wonder, the monarchical African leadership lost to colonialism. Third, the supervisory role of the king in most cases was not adequate for the entire kingdom. Strong men, women and emerging potential leaders were sold as slaves. Africa became vulnerable to any attacks and loss of great leaders who would develop the continent spiritually and socio-economically. Study the two figures of the organization of the African society below.

---

5. Elliston, *Home Grown Leaders*, 22–23.

ORGANIZATION OF THE AFRICAN SOCIETY

In traditional African society status and roles are separated as his or her highness status, clan leadership, family and individual society members. Families and clans are ethnic groups of specific society members. The kingdom is more influential than clan, tribe or family and individuals in African society. Therefore, its influence is more respected in the society than individuals'. This is why in figure 1 below; the kingdom is represented by a bigger circle; then, clan/tribe and lastly, the family and individual society members. This is according to the area of jurisdiction of the status and the role these society leaders can play in African society.

Figure 2: *A Traditional African Leadership Social Structure*

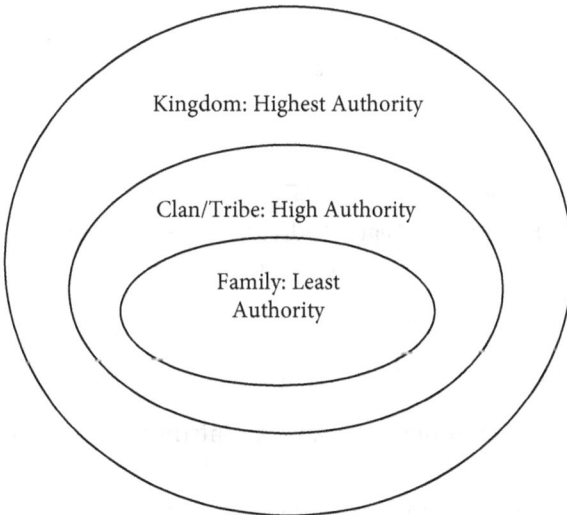

In traditional African society the highest authority is the king or the chief; his or her royal highness. Clan or tribal leaders are next in authority. The highest authority oversees other traditional authorities. These traditional leaders play very significant roles in the welfare of the society. They are expected to provide protection to the immediate community

they oversee; give traditional training or orientation to the new generation about their kingdom, clan and family. The king or queen organizes
his/her work through his/her subordinates in the structure. In the African
setting, line of authority is always top-down. The family community is
the least authority. No individual family member makes a family decision
without consulting with the elders in the family lineage.

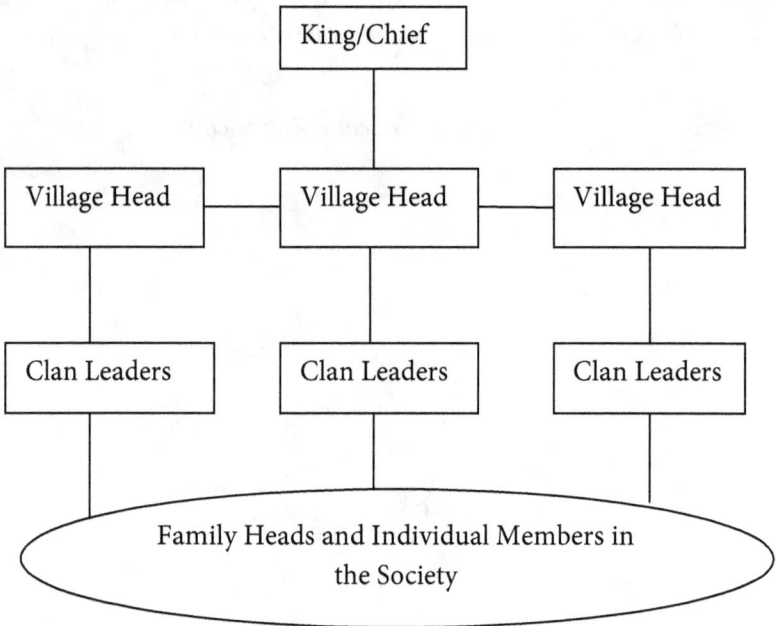

Figure 3: Traditional African Administrative Structure

During monarchical system of governance in Africa, there were no fixed
political boundaries. Or rather people did not respect boundaries. People
would migrate from one kingdom into another without any boundary
restrictions. The boundaries would be shifted at anytime. There used to be
wars between kingdoms, tribes and clans. Whoever lost at war did not just
lose the war; but people, kingdom, and power; unlike the contemporary
world where one would just lose the war and power. It is also imperative

to understand that there was no consideration of developing emerging Christian and political leadership outside the royal family. The potentially emerging leaders from outside the royal family trees were sold during slave trade. However, the coming of the missionaries to Africa brought peace and social stability. The fighting tribes were brought to reconciliation and slavery was abolished; although fighting did not completely cease. The missionaries fought against slavery and tribal wars in Africa. Since the African kingdoms were vast, control and governance became big challenges to the monarchical system of governance. This was the opportunity for colonizers. They divided the continent into administrative and manageable countries. Since there were no leaders yet developed to take the challenges of leading and ruling those countries, the probability for the colonizers to lead and rule Africa was high. Then, they led Africa and exploited its resources as it is the case for every leadership in Africa.

The monarchical system of leadership in Africa lost to colonization. Africa was colonized in the eighteenth and nineteenth centuries. Kingdoms, tribes and clans which broke during the slave trade never reunited. The slave trade and colonization finished up monarchical leadership in Africa and brought about master-servant leadership which was more like monarchical leadership that never demonstrated the character of a Christian leader. The similarity between monarchical and colonial leadership (master-servant) was its characteristics of dictatorship, oppression, and failure to recognize the potential emerging leaders from within indigenous members of the kingdom or the society in general. It was also characterized by master-servant relationships between the colonial leaders (masters) and the natives (servants). The natives lost their natural identity and leadership recognition. They no longer ruled themselves. They depended on their colonial masters for spiritual guidance, social and political governance and economic support. This model did not provide a better model for Christian leadership development. The model of Christian leadership is servanthood leadership. In Africa this model of leadership can only be found in the scriptures; even the European missionaries did not exemplify it.

Leadership paradigm shift from colonial to post-colonial was through party politics which had presidents, governors and prime ministers as community and national leaders. Consequently, this created social and administrative structures that were unfitting to the African society. This model also fell short of the characteristics expected of Christian leadership development. However, the church borrowed much from this model of leadership and paternalism was the result. The church borrowed systems of recruitment and selection of leaders; and master-servant leadership development from the colonial leadership.

After colonization, came independence in the mid twentieth century. African nations became independent of colonial powers and natives ruled themselves from the colonial masters. The independent African leaders were later characterized by intimidation, autocratic rule, single party system of governance and lack of transparency and accountability. However, the strength of the independent African leaders was state sovereignty, national solidarity and national identity. At least unity and peace prevailed in most African countries more than it is today. The greatest challenge of the independent African states was the exercise of freedom and human rights. Nonetheless, the church still had no good model to emulate from the independent African leaders. This was because many leaders were not transparent and accountable to the nations. They were notorious and politically motivated to the point of executing the innocent emerging potential leaders. They made no difference with the monarchies who sold the emerging potential leaders to slave traders. For example, in Malawi, Muwalo Ncgumayo was executed on political reasons when he challenged the then political leadership. The situation terrorized the emerging leaders to challenge the prevailing social, political and spiritual leadership; even when the incumbent leaders were wrong and incompetent.

The monarchical type of leadership failed Africa to recognize the love of God for one another. The leaders were characterized by their thirst for wars, self-ambitions and extension of their kingdom boundaries through conquests. They were highly influenced by their trade in guns from the slave traders and colonizers. They did not faithfully serve the people as God intended for them. They did not realize that they were leaders by God's will. They assumed the position of a Master and their followers were either recognized as slaves or servants. There was no spiritual, social, economic and emerging leadership development for both spiritual and socio-political institutions.

The post-colonial leadership was characterized by dictatorship, undemocratic, oppression, execution, unaccountability and lack of transparency. The political, economic and spiritual development in African countries in some instances was described as underdeveloped, unstable and poor. In some cases, for example, in Malawi, Jehovah's Witnesses were denied freedom of worship few years after independence. In fact, Jehovah's Witnesses were not allowed to worship freely in Malawi because of their low profile in political activities until after the introduction of multi-party democracy in 1994 when Malawi had its first democratic general elections. Therefore, the African independent political leadership never provided a model for Christian leadership development. All potentially emerging leaders both in politics and in Christianity did not show up for leadership development; they feared for their lives and sought for political asylum in neighbouring countries. For example, Thabo Mbeki of South Africa spent some time in Zambia as a political asylum seeker, Kanyama Chiume of Malawi was in Tanzania as a political refugee for several years; just to mention a few.

DEMOCRATIC AFRICAN LEADERSHIP MODELS

The current democratic leaders in Africa are almost reverting to open-ended term of presidential office which is characterized by dictatorship, oppression, and lack of transparency as it was in the previous regime. The topic that dominates political forums in most African states in the late twentieth century and early the twenty-first century is the third term or open-ended term for the president. The proponents of third presidential term are actually proposing for life presidency that was voted out at the introduction of multiparty democracy in Zambia and Malawi. However, churches, civil societies and some politicians fight against that kind of democracy. The proponents of third or open-ended presidential term tried their luck through constitutional reviews, but to no avail. In some countries, for example, in Malawi and Zambia, when the third term deal failed, the outgoing leaders imposed the political party leaders on people as presidential candidates to take political leadership positions after them. The reason for this was for the incoming president to shield them from corruption cases which were prevalent and are actually prosecuted for the same. Nevertheless, the imposed leaders did not succumb to the desires of their predecessors. The predecessors' desire was to rule through the imposed political leaders and that the corruption cases should not surface when they retire from politics.

This kind of leadership is not only in political forums, but in the Christian leadership of the twenty-first century as well. The Christian leadership in Africa has greatly been influenced by political system of governance. The people in the church advocate for democratic system in electing the church leadership. Unfortunately, the egalitarian system is adopted in the church government without critically examining its implications to the biblical perspective of Christian leadership, African social structure and the mission of the church.

The western democracy is not fitting in the African socio-political and administrative structures. African political system takes after monarchical leadership structure where the king is the sole ruler and leader and gives commands to his/her subjects. This system gives no room for potential emerging Christian or political leadership development outside the royal family. African social structure is such that the king is the sole leader. Naturally, one rules until death do us part. Then, the next leader is chosen from the same family. The provision of electing leaders randomly from the society other than from the royal family is strange to the development of African leadership structure; though it has been in Africa for about fifty years now. This is one reason for vote apathy in African politics. Some Africans do not really find reasons for voting after all leaders are obviously known to becoming from those born leaders (royal family).

The Old and the New Testaments are clear that God appointed leaders for his people according to what he intended those leaders for and what he saw in their hearts. Even when Jesus came, he appointed those whom he designated apostles to lead the church after him (Mark 3:13–15). The apostles also when they wanted someone to replace Judah Iscariot, they did not elect the apostle through democratic ballot. Yet, this does not mean that democratic system of governance is evil as some may suppose. There is nothing wrong with democratic system of governance. Where the church needs to be careful is its practicability in the church setting and mission. Should the church leaders be elected through a democratic ballot? How can we properly apply the biblical models of appointing leaders through the elders (National Church Leaders)? What should be the procedures and criteria of appointing a person to church leadership in Africa? The biblical method of electing leaders that is similar to democratic ballot is casting lots. But casting lots was more unbiased and efficient method than casting vote in the democratic system. It was difficult to predict the result of the elections in casting lots method, compared to present democratic elections; that even before votes are cast one can predict the results of the elections.

BIBLICAL MODEL OF ELECTING CHURCH LEADERSHIP

The African political leadership whether monarchical, colonial, post-colonial or democratic does not provide a good model for the Christian leadership development to emulate. It is culturally unfitting in the African social and administrative structures. The church needs to critically follow the biblical way of electing or appointing leaders to positions in the church and the society. Leaders in the church are servants rather than bosses or masters. They must be led by the Holy Spirit in serving others; they ought to serve people with humility and must be accountable to God for whatever they do in their leadership. Acts 1; 6 and I Timothy 3 set the minimum required qualifications for Christian leaders. Some qualifications are; s/he must be full of the Holy Spirit, good reputation, integrity, must not be a novice, a person of wisdom and etc. Those who qualify must be appointed by the board of elders to positions needing leaders. Democracy in the African society seems to be both incompatible with the existing African cultures and problematic in political institutions as well as in the church. The African social and administrative structures for leadership in the church and the society seems incompatible to the Western understanding of the same, where democracy has gone through the process of evolution the past two hundred years or so. Africa is still struggling with the adjustment to democratic leadership structures that work efficiently in western countries. The concept of democracy hasn't been developed enough to provide a good model for Christian leadership in Africa both in the church and the socio-political institutions. There are a lot of cliques and fighting leading to leadership crisis and conflicts on the African continent. For instance, 2007 and 2008 general elections in Kenya and Zimbabwe respectively, do they reflect an understanding of democracy? Are the solutions offered to both situations democratically acceptable? Does the situation in Kenya or Zimbabwe provide democratic values worthy emulation by the church? Both cases have been characterized by rejection of the election results, clinging to leadership status without the majority mandate as required in democratic procedures and sharing one's power with someone who did not deserve it democratically. Certainly, this system has failed to provide the right model of leadership for the church. Nonetheless, it is important to learn lessons from such a system of electing leaders; even in the church setting. We must recognize that leaders in the church are appointed by God according to the purpose for which they are appointed. Nowhere in the Bible were Christian leaders elected through democratic process. However, casting of lots in the Bible may imply the casting of vote to determine the winner or appointed leaders for the church or any organization in the society.

Much of the church's and social problems in the society today emanate from leaders who were elected democratically but cannot deliver because they cannot meet the required qualifications of the Christian leader set in the Bible and the purpose for which they are elected. Christian leaders are uniquely called to fulfil what God wants for his people. Many other scholars may argue that the view portrayed in this chapter demeans the power of prayer and decmocracy before and during elections for godly church leadership. This is not so. Does prayer nullify the set standards of appointing church leaders that God himself set? When we read the Bible where leaders were appointed to take over positions in the church leadership, we find that people prayed and God led them through the process to appointing church leaders who served Him and the people well; and of course, some did not. As much as we may appreciate social and human development that has taken place between then and now, and that many things have evolved; yet the democratic model for electing church and society leaders is nowhere in the Bible nor has it worked better in the secular political organizations. Leadership in the church is by appointment and objective determination of the gift of the Holy Spirit. Majority must rule principle is incompatible with theocracy and biblical democracy. Theocracy and biblical democracy provides that people should be appointed and lead according to the purpose of their calling to leadership ministry and the gifting of the Holy Spirit.

AFFIRMING THE ROLE OF THE HOLY SPIRIT IN DEVELOPING EMERGING CHURCH LEADERS

The role of the Holy Spirit is noteworthy in developing the emerging Christian leaders in the church in Africa. The challenges of Christian leadership in any growing church cannot be overcome without giving the Holy Spirit a prominent position in developing Christian leaders. Christian leadership development is a process of identifying, recruiting, training and deploying the potential leaders for what they were called and empowered. Christian leadership development should depend on the role of the Holy Spirit during recruitment, selection, and training of leaders.

They should also lead the flock of God as models, giving credence to the Chief Shepherd; Jesus Christ. The issues of culture and traditions can only be dealt with effectively when the Holy Spirit becomes a supreme leader of the process of developing Christian leadership both in Africa and in any society.

People are glued to culture and traditions. They feel comfortable, united and related to each other through culture and traditions. In most African societies, people live as communities bound in their customs and cultures that apply to their real life situation and therefore depend on one another for finances and other social amenities. Because of the community life in Africa, leadership was by inheritance from family line and majority support (royal family appointment). The consideration was placed on age and relationships in the family tree and not on abilities, spiritual gifts and the fruit of the Spirit. However, the immediate family was required to qualify the appointee for wisdom to govern the kingdom or the family. This is typical of traditional African leadership. This system has no consideration of skills, abilities, fruit and the gift of the spirit and the calling to leadership. Consequently, emerging leaders who do not belong to the family tree of the kingdom have no chance for consideration for Christian leadership development. No individual decision is valid in such societies.

Therefore to impact such a society spiritually, culturally and socially for the transformation of behavior in the society is both essential and difficult. Some cultural relationships are detrimental to Christian leadership development process. The culture of the people determines their behavior and working relationships. The role of the Holy Spirit to bring about the desired transformation in such societies is both a challenge and indispensable. Church growth cannot be realized unless emerging potential Christian leaders have been given chance to develop their potentialities according to their calling and challenges. Emerging potential leaders need to be given leadership assignments that are challenging both spiritually and socially, in order for them to develop their abilities and exercise their spiritual gifts and the fruit of the Spirit. It is necessary therefore to overcome cultural barriers to emerging Christian leadership development by emphasizing biblical principles of electing and developing Christian leaders.

In Acts 6:1-4, we notice the conflict between cultural identity and the church work. Indicators of church growth and the role of the Holy Spirit in the emerging Christian leaders are conflicting. The church grew and incorporated people who were non Jews and had different traditions to those of the Jews. Thus, the church required Christian leaders who were born again, spirit-filled and impartial. The people who served on tables were perhaps men of wisdom and of good reputation. Yet cultural identity did matter in that early church and caused disparity between the Hebraic and Grecian Jews. There was also a threat to the growth of the church administratively. In addition, it implied that capacity building was necessary since the church had to grow inevitably. "When the church grew, Grecian Jews among them complained against the Hebraic Jews because their widows were neglected in the daily distribution of food" (Acts 6:1). Christian leaders who were without the Holy Spirit and wisdom became partial in their execution of duties. Therefore, defining the roles of the Holy Spirit in that situation was just as important for four main reasons. *First*, the role of the Holy Spirit in the recruitment of the emerging Christian leaders was vital. People find solace when the Holy Spirit is given the rightful place, even in the social concerns of Christians such as daily distribution of food (Acts 6). *Second*, the role of the Holy Spirit is essential for selection of the Christian leaders according to the fruit and the gift of the Spirit, experience and integrity. Christian leaders are the people who give direction to the entire church community through vision casting and strategically planning toward church growth and leadership development. Hence, they should be men and women of vision, focused mind, integrity and impartiality.

The vision of the church must be birthed from the inspiration of the Holy Spirit and interaction with the social life of the society through learning and studying their culture. Leaders must get the vision of the church from the Holy Spirit. As Harris Lees notes that the vision of the church does not spring from the leader's mind or from out of the blue, but from reading the scriptures and from reflection on the contemporary needs of the church, the community, and the larger world.[6] The church is God's entity, in developing the vision of the church. Leadership ought to keep abreast of its deliberate intentions to leaders of every church department spiritually and socially. Members need to know what and how they ought to do things for the well being of the church and the entire society. That is, the timeframe, framework of the activities and the reasons for engaging in such activities.

6. Lee, *Effective Church Leadership: A Practical Sourcebook*, 179.

To get a clear and realistic vision of the church does not only depend on reading the scriptures as suggested by Lee, but illumination of the scriptures by the Holy Spirit to give the understanding of the scriptures to the reader so that the leader can lead the church according to the will of God. Further, integration of spiritual and contemporary political and socio-economic needs of the community requires the wisdom and knowledge of the Holy Spirit-filled Christian leader. The Holy Spirit gives the leader faith and courage to meet both spiritual and empirical contemporary needs efficiently and effectively with the church resources.

Third, theological training of Christian leaders is just as important to the church growth as proclamation of the gospel. The growth of the church certainly depends on well theologically trained leaders who may take care of the flock and develop other leaders after them. "Effective leaders maintain a learning posture throughout life."[7] When leaders stop learning what they continue to do is only ignorance and spreading problems without solutions. Leaders who continue learning both formally and informally grow with the knowledge of congregations or organizations they lead and serve respectively and practically. Problems in the church ministry are inevitable and they need fresh and situational approach each time they incur. Therefore, continuous theological training and learning on the part of the leader and his flock is crucial. However, the role of the Holy Spirit in such learning and training is indispensable. Continuous theological training and learning enables the incumbent Christian leaders to learn and seek new approaches to the prevailing growth challenges and problems of the church. Principle – centred leaders listen to others and learn through both their eyes and ears.[8] And the Apostle Paul in his leadership development told his apprentice, Timothy, that the things he saw him doing he should entrust them to faithful men who would be qualified to teach others (2 Tim 2:2).

Any theological training of Christian leadership that ignores the Holy Spirit is ruining its basic requirements for church growth and social and human development of the community. The Holy Spirit makes Christian leaders effective. In fact, Christian leaders should be baptized with the Holy Spirit before they are deployed to assume Christian leadership responsibilities of the church.

7. Roberts, *Lessons in Leadership: Fifty Respected Evangelical Leaders share their Wisdom in Ministry*, 72.

8. Covey, *Principle- Centred Leadership*, 33.

Fourth, the Holy Spirit should lead in the deployment of the trained Christian leaders to the mission field. "Set apart for me Barnabas and Saul for the work to which I have called them" (Acts 13:2). The Holy Spirit should give direction as to where the people of God must go. Theological training institutions and seminaries should take heed to the direction the Holy Spirit gives to the church for leadership development and deployment. Unfortunately, in most theological training institutions today, the concept of training leaders for the universal church seems to be diminishing. The concentration of our theological training is mainly for meeting local church or denominational needs; what a mediocre perception! The big picture and meaning of the universal church must remain the focus of Christian leadership development whether in Africa or anywhere else.

BIBLICAL IMAGES OF LEADERSHIP FOR THE CHURCH IN AFRICAN CULTURAL CONTEXT

"The contemporary leadership in the world contends for status, domination and control."[9] This type of leadership does nothing with servant leadership. In African and many other cultural contexts, the position a person assumes in the society makes him/her a leader. Examples of such leaders are kings, political and traditional community leaders. This also determines the roles a particular person plays in the particular society. In most cases, the relationship between a leader and followers is that of master-servant. This is typical of the secular kind of leadership in Africa and anywhere else. The servant is always answerable to the master and is treated as such. The master in this case, is a Christian church leader and the servant is the follower or member of a certain religion or church. The servant obeys the orders from the master and in most cases does not argue for conditions. The issue of servant-hood is nonexistent in such cultural church leadership context. The apostle Paul describes this situation very clearly in his letter to the church at Ephesus (Eph 6:5, 9). "Christians may have the feeling that the church is undemocratic because some church leaders try to take the role of God."[10] God is the Master and Christian leaders are servants serving both God and their

---

9. Osei-Mensah, *Wanted Servant Leadership*, 10.
10. Pembamoyo, *June 2006, Nation Newspaper*, 7.

fellow servants in the kingdom. The status of a master should be left for God; while all Christian leaders assume the role of a servant.

It is assumed that the transition of leadership in Africa from colonialism to independence and the system of political governance in the independence regime influenced the church in Africa. Christian leadership assumed the role of a boss and master-servant. They became untouchable church elite.

Some African countries got independence early in the nineteen sixties from the colonial masters and others later. During colonization, Africans were servants to colonial masters. The African cultural way of raising traditional leaders was thwarted and dominated by the Western systems of making leaders except in very few countries that remained kingdoms where the Western impact was not as much. As such, their influence was insignificant for developing emerging Christian leaders in Africa. However, those kingdoms embraced nominal Christianity; until now the kings in Swaziland and Morocco do not follow Christian ethics and morals.

History teaches that missionaries preceded colonialists. But the colonialists partitioned Africa and took over dominion from traditional African leaders. Various western denominations also partitioned Africa or tribes according to their belief systems and denominational lines. This is why we have Anglicans, Roman Catholics, Pentecostals, Presbyterians and so forth. So, Africa was divided both politically and religiously. Missionaries and traditional African leaders relinquished their powers to colonial masters. Early Christian missionaries to Africa came from Europe. Then, the Arabs followed and introduced Islam in most countries in the north, west and along the East Coast of Africa. And the Christian leadership in most African countries was master-servant type of leadership because of the influence of European colonization and Arab slave traders. The western missionaries established parishes as central administrative centres. The parishioners acted like administrators and masters. Indigenous Christians were serving these parishioners and not the other way around. However, this type did not demonstrate the desired model of Christian leadership as asserted by Jesus Christ (John 13:13). That leadership lacked the attitude and component of humility in their leadership character development.

The leadership model the colonialists, missionaries and Arabs introduced on African continent was that of master-servant. No wonder, the consequences of that leadership was paternalism, nominal Christianity and leadership development did not consider emerging potential leaders in the African society and the church. Both the colonial system and early denominationalism in Africa did not provide the Christian model of servanthood leadership development. Hence, the church leadership was master-servant. The transition of government system from colonial powers to independence in the mid and late twentieth century carried with it dictatorship rule just to force master-servant relationships amongst people. Leadership influenced the church polity in many ways. *First*, most political leaders were appointed to their positions by the president or prime minister. The functions of such offices were politically biased and motivated. Since the people in positions were appointed, they worked to please their masters; presidents or prime ministers. "The transition from an authoritarian to egalitarian form of government is a major paradigm shift for any society."[11] This is the church's strength to follow biblical trend of electing church leaders through appointment to serve God, the master. The master-servant leadership dominated the church leadership as well in most parts of Africa in that century. Almost all positions in the church were by appointments. It is a wonder that most churches in Africa now follow democratic system of election of the church leaders. However, the churches that are democratic in nature do not consider spiritual gifts and the fruit of the Spirit in appointing or electing church leaders; nor those that are undemocratic. The qualifications for church leadership positions are no less than that of the secular institutions. Such leaders mostly, do not demonstrate servant leadership qualities that the church needs. The democratically elected Christian leaders feel they deserve it because of the electorate vote. They do not consider it as a privilege. This is unfortunate part to hear about Christian leadership in Africa. They are mere workers not ministers who have passion for God and compassion for the people they serve. "Funds were solicited in America to pay national workers who ministered under the watchful gaze, albeit beneficent control of the missionaries."[12] Christian leaders are not mere leaders, but called to be co-leaders together with

11. Ihonvbere, *Economic Crisis, Civil Society & Democratization: The Case of Zambia*, 286.

12. Dempster et al., *Called & Empowered: Global Missions in Pentecostal Perspective*, 210.

God (1 Cor 3:9); therefore, they need to collaborate with him in their leadership style.

The church of the twentieth century emulated the secular system of recruiting and selecting leaders. In reality, almost all churches were first led by the white European missionaries. This gave Africans an impression that missionaries are white Europeans. Nevertheless, this impression is diminishing in the modern Christian generation. Unfortunately, some of those missionaries never gave power back to the indigenous church leaders even when the locals were able to lead their indigenous churches. The reason for not trusting African Christian leadership was the missionaries' failure to develop it. They did not develop local Christian leaders in Africa. Paternalism was the result of that failure. Some churches even now are not autonomous *per se.*

There has been enormous growth of master-servant leadership model until the late twentieth century for most churches including some Pentecostal churches in Africa. In the late twentieth century, African states adopted the democratic system of government. The church also started electing its leaders using democratic instruments. Consequently, development of biblical images of Christian leadership in Africa is collapsing. Is the shift from egalitarian political models to appointment biblical models live up to reality? Just as the master-servant leadership evolved from colonialism and independent African political leaders; so, also church leadership in Africa should shift to a system of appointing leaders following more closely to biblical model where leaders are appointed and commissioned (Acts 1:16–25; 6; 13). The church may not necessarily cast lots but pray for the appointment of church leaders and appoint them basing on biblically set qualifications. Those who may fulfil the basic requirements should be scrutinized by the serving leadership and eventually appoint them into church leadership.

Politically, the democratization process has not only impacted political, social and economic institutions, but the church too. Most African leaders in the church are elected democratically. In most cases these leaders do not make themselves accountable to people they lead in the disguise that they are responsible and accountable to God. As a result, the society and the church are a mess due to irresponsible leaders. Christian leaders despite that they are responsible to God, the view l also agree, they must demonstrate to the society that they are God's trustees (Heb 5:1–3).

Most governments in Africa are not responsible and accountable to people. This is one reason why there is much corruption on the continent and the poor are becoming poorer. The Christian leadership is robed of its servant-hood style demonstrated by Jesus Christ. In an egalitarian government if a leader is not responsible and accountable to people, they vote him/her out of office even before the expiry period of that office through recalling, referendum or impeachment processes. But in the church today, corruption is tolerated. Christian leadership with servanthood characteristics are farfetched in the contemporary society.

Servant leaders are people oriented rather than mere observers of *modus operandi*. A servant leader cares for the needy.[13] Christian leaders ought to view leadership as a challenge to carnal pressure of prestige, pride and power. Christian leadership must take after Jesus Christ the author of our faith. "Who being in the very nature God, did not consider equality with God something to be grasped, but made himself nothing, taking the very nature of a *servant*" (italics mine) (Phil 2:6–7). Christian leadership in African cultural setting needs spiritual transformation and a paradigm shift from autocratic, master-servant, and egalitarian type of leadership to appointed servant-leadership. They must acknowledge their appointments as a privilege God has accorded them; not their achievement. The Bible hardly provides a model of egalitarian leadership. God is the one responsible for appointing leaders through the standing church leadership to lead his flock. However, it is important to develop a system of electing church leaders that is compatible with the biblical models rather than depending on egalitarian system as if it is the only best. Christian leaders ought to understand the biblical foundation of their ministry.[14] Ministers should understand that they are servant leaders; just as was the Lord Jesus Christ.

In the African context, servant leadership is an asset and a necessity. Servant leadership is people oriented through development of interpersonal relationships which comes natural to Africans because of communalism and extended family relations. But this is not the case with most contemporary African leaderships today whether political, corporate and spiritual. The followers are treated as servants and individuals even in the church or Para church organizations. The major problem of Christian

13. Bowling, *Grace-Full Leadership: Understanding the Heart of a Christian Leader*, 25.

14. McBride, *How To Lead Small Groups*, 13.

leadership development in Africa is in the exercise of authority and power and the system of recruiting, selecting and developing culturally emerging leaders. Christian leaders in the church were supposed to be recruited, selected and appointed from mature Christians who are full of the Spirit, men and women of good reputation and wisdom.

The Bible has explicitly cited four images that signify a typical Christian church leader as he ought to reflect himself while leading the flock of God. The Bible is crystal clear in that a Christian leader must be a servant, shepherd, steward and harvester to the flock. He/she ought to lead in love, patience and gentleness with those who cannot cope up quickly with the Christian lifestyle and by example just as the Chief Shepherd, Jesus Christ did. Although He was God He became a servant like us and demonstrated all godliness for us to emulate. "You call me teacher and Lord, and rightly so, for that is what I am. Now that I, your Teacher and Lord, have washed your feet, you also should wash one another's feet" (John 13:13–14). This scenario expresses Jesus' expectation of a Christian leader, how he ought to conduct herself or himself in humility as s/he influences the flock to follow her/him as s/he follows Christ. This is more than just having a status in the church or occupying a place of authority in ministry or the society. Actually, it is a reality of biblical image of servanthood. Therefore, Christian leaders have to emulate Jesus' example of leadership and the church should elect church leadership based on the qualifications set in the Bible by God himself.

Christian leaders who fail to understand Jesus' leadership model of servanthood, seldom realize their position in ministry and the potential in others who follow them in the church. Usually such leaders consider themselves better than others. The result is that such church leaders do not develop the potential in others into full realization for the cause of the gospel and social development of the society. The Bible teaches that consider others better than you. They place the biblical values at wrong premise. They look at themselves as star performers not star developers and do not recognize and consider diversity in Christian leadership calling. God gave diverse spiritual gifts to the church to prepare God's people for works of service (Eph. 4:12). "Moses felt that since he was God's chosen leader for the people, he alone could do the task; he alone must shoulder the responsibility. . . ."[15] This concept of Christian leader-

15. Osei-Mensah, *Wanted Servant Leaders*, 15.

ship encourages the disparity between the professional and laity church leadership. "Many churches suffer from a general passivity of the (laity) people of God."[16] This is why there are wars and economic crises in African countries and unnecessary political conflicts in the church. In Africa, men and women want to be star performers.

Certainly, star performers do not embrace the full teaching of Jesus Christ about Christian leadership development. These are the leaders who serve for their positions because they have been elected to such an office and not the functions for which they have been elected. The attitude of stewardship and servant hood has no place in their hearts and plans of the church development or growth. In other words, they just fulfil a duty in the work of God and not ministry. But Christian leaders are servants, shepherds, stewards and harvesters who carefully look after the flock of God that none should perish and are people-oriented because they are also responsible to God and the people they lead.

The leader portrayed in biblical images ought to have love and compassion for the lost, passion for God, commitment to ministry and humility as his basic attitudes. The highest value of such leaders is the better life of the flock they lead, rather than their personal achievements and welfare. It is, therefore, of paramount importance that such leaders ought to be esteemed highly in the church and the society.

In African context, the images of leadership take secular viewpoint; where a leader is a chief or king. Sometimes Africans use analogies to describe leadership. This is expressed in the stories about animals ascribed to the leaders. In essence, African metaphors are both good and bad for Christian leadership; for example, the lion represents strong or powerful leader in African context. This is inline with the use of the same when it represents Christ in the Bible. It is important also to understand that a lion intimidates other animals in the jungle. This means that African Christian leaders ought to realize that they should not intimidate their leadership apprentices. Nevertheless, Christian leadership in Africa needs transformation of life so that their use of power and authority may be conformed to the likeness of Christ and how He used power in fulfilling His ministry requirements on earth. In fact, Jesus came to transform people from impotent to potential leaders the master can use for His own glory.

---

16. Elliston, *Home Grown Leaders*, 20.

BASIC ELEMENTS OF LEADERSHIP IN AFRICA

The *what* of leadership is the study of basic elements of Christian leadership. This part discusses the importance of self-awareness, cultural identity and calling to ministry. The study of these elements is crucial in Christian leadership development from African perspective. The leadership in the church is different from secular leadership in that the church's products are people; and therefore, relationships and transformed life are imperative for African leadership development.

a. Self–Awareness

"Understanding leadership begins with attention to who we are and not just what we do."[17] The question of who we are is very important and can have two aspects: integrity and our perception of the people we serve. Integrity may talk more of who we are before God and the people we serve as leaders. Integrity talks about accountability and transparency of leadership. It describes the character of a leader. Leaders must be accountable for the trust to God and the people they serve. Integrity calls for transparency, accountability and responsibility both to God and the people as Lindsell notes that leadership is a gift, a responsibility and a position of trust.[18] Trustees are stewards. In this case, Christian leaders are trustees of God's flock. How they lead the flock towards God matters most to both God and the people they serve. The apostle Peter said, ". . . not lording it over those entrusted to you, but being examples to the flock" (1 Pet. 5: 3). As God's trustees, Christian African leaders ought to be faithful and integrity. Responsibility, accountability and transparency should be their highest desire. Leaders arc accountable to God and to the people they serve (Heb. 13: 17). Leaders should lead the people of God with integrity, love and truthfulness because they will give an account of their work of leadership to God on the last day. "Integrity is the heart of character."[19] Leading with consciousness is therefore, a necessity and crucial for Christian African leadership. Our leadership should be necessitated with a responsibility

17. Bowling, *Grace-Full Leadership: Understanding the Heart of a Christian Leader*, 14.

18. Lindsell, *Relationships: Jesus Style*, 24.

19. Clinton, *The Making of a Leader: Recognizing the Lessons and Stages of Leadership Development*, 58.

we have before God and His flock. Therefore, character development in the life of a Christian is cardinal.

The leader's perception of the people he leads is significant. Sometimes Christian leaders are tempted to look at people in their churches as if they were their property or servants. The danger with such perception is that you are not responsible to anyone. The people we lead in the church are God's people. He watches over them day and night, and meets their needs. "See that you do not look down on one of these little ones. For I tell you that their angels in heaven always see the face of my Father in heaven" (Matt. 18:10). That is why it is important that leaders should have good perception and relationship with God before they become leaders of His people. The leader's relationship with God as his Saviour and Lord is crucial and a basic requirement for Christian African leadership development. The people we lead in the church are valuable in the eyes of God who has called us to the ministry of leadership. The transformed life of a Christian as s/he becomes a leader of God's flock is of paramount importance. The value we give to the people we lead in the church makes us effective leaders of God's people or not. Therefore, Christian African leaders ought to be aware of their integrity, transformed life and responsibility over God's flock. ". . . We believe that our leadership effectiveness is strengthened through an increase of self- and other awareness."[20]

b. Cultural Identity

A Christian leader needs identification with people s/he leads. Christian Leaders ought to incarnate in the people's culture, core values, and societies needs. This will enable the leader to study and learn the beliefs and values of the society s/he leads. Emerging African Christian leaders are informal rather than formal in the way they learn leadership skills. They are not recognized by their status in the society but by their people-oriented skills, Christ-like character and passion for God and compassion for people. Their role in the society is always appreciated and felt by the members of the society; not by lording them but becoming an example in Christian life (1 Pet 5:1–5). Traditional African leaders develop others through apprenticeship and mentoring processes. The apprentice observes how the kingdom is run by observation and incarnation.

20. Lee, *Effective Church Leadership: A Practical Sourcebook*, 55.

Every church or society has its own spiritual and social needs. An African Christian leader should study peoples' needs, mobilize the resources and take people there. Many leaders politically or spiritually have condemned people just because they have different worldview or opinion on some matters about their culture, values and priorities. Anthropologically, Christian leaders study people holistically and provide guidance for the people to get there where their needs can be met by the most culturally accepted and effective strategy. The unique cultural identity of African leadership is its submission to the majority view, rather than pursuing individual's goal. An African is identified culturally with the ethnic group of his/her clan.

Christian church leaders should be indigenous in leading the worship service in the church, developing interpersonal relationships and strategies for developing potential emerging church leaders. Churches should be indigenous not only geographically, linguistically, but in leadership and finances too. The Christian church leaders should be training indigenous church members the methods of raising funds for the church to avoid donor dependence syndrome which the previous African church leadership regime overlook. The indigenous African church should be characterized by self-support, self-propagation, self-theologizing and self-government. However, it is also important to understand that the selves that have been discussed here do not make a Christian church leader in Africa and elsewhere to be independent of God. Its God who sustains every self defined in this text.

c. Calling to Leadership Ministry in Africa

The Christian African leader should be aware of the spiritual gifts God has given to the church for leadership development. The church is a corporate organization of God. It has diversity of gifts for diversity of ministerial leadership in diverse cultures. The uniqueness of an African leader is more vivid in the church than in any other organization by the way s/he leads and value the people God has entrusted under his/her charge. The fruit of the Spirit is a unique identity of Christian African leaders in the church as a community. Unless the African church leadership appreciates the diversity in the church giftedness, the fruit of the spirit will not serve any purpose in that community; and God's provision of various gifts in the church may be void. If the church wants to maximize the leadership potential in Africa, it has to learn to delegate responsibilities to members of the church basing on their spiritual gifts and the fruit of the spirit. It must develop Christian leadership that is fitting to African culture and situation. The church is a unique organization because of the spiritual gifts God has provided for its leadership development or church growth. "The most grateful compliment we can pay our God is to fulfil and optimize our uniqueness."[21] Our uniqueness in Christian leadership is solely in making use of the spiritual gifts and the fruit of the spirit as we lead others to God.

The church in Africa can certainly solve many of its problems related to relationship conflicts and proclamation of the gospel through effective delegation of responsibilities of the church to people in accordance with their spiritual leadership gifts and manifestation of the fruit of the spirit (Exod 18:13–27). However, it should be realized also that this way of doing things in the church will go against systems of elections which most likely disregard spiritual gifts and the fruit of the spirit. Seldom do people in the church governments elect leaders according to their spiritual leadership gifts. "In the final analysis we must always remember that our greatest source of worth as leaders should come from the knowledge that we are known by God . . . ."[22] Traditional means of raising leaders in Africa has no regard to spiritual giftedness and the fruit of the spirit in most cases, whether in politics or in the church. This is why it is important to understand the need for transformation of personality through new birth for Christian leaders.

THE HOW OF AFRICAN LEADERSHIP

Leadership is generally defined as an influence. Yet, how that influence impacts the followers is another issue. Leaders influence followers either through their leadership style or the way they exercise their powers and authority in leadership ministry. In African context, the exercise of power and authority is critical and limited by the model Christians ought to emulate from Christ. Christians are leaders after their Chief leader—Jesus Christ. If Christian leaders in Africa fail to understand how Jesus led His flock, that is, He humbled Himself and became a servant of the people

21. Smith, *Leading with Integrity: Competence with Christian Character*, 101.

22. McIntosh and Rima, *Overcoming the Dark Side of Leadership: The Paradox of Personal Dysfunction*, 205.

He served; then, Christian African leadership ministry is lording over the flock of God. This kind of leadership is contrary to Christian leadership expectation and an unacceptable in the church. Christian leaders lead as servants not as bosses in their functions. Since African leadership development is informal, leaders are developed through mentoring and apprenticeship. Therefore, the leadership style, power and authority they ought to demonstrate should certainly take after Jesus' style of leadership.

In African context, politically, leadership style that overruled the continent for the past centuries had been autocratic. Some church leaders after learning from political leaders and environment, they also became autocratic and thereby bringing about nominal Christianity, divisions and uncaring leaders in the church because people followed them out of fear. An autocratic leader always thinks he is the best leader; and that he alone can direct the activities of the church or the nation satisfactorily and that, because of his great knowledge and ability, the church can achieve the best results through him/her alone. This is typical of most African leaders. They cling to position of authority until their death. Nevertheless, it is imperative to learn that the trend of African leaders clinging to position of power is diminishing in the modern Africa.

Lawrence Gangel observes that some leaders because of their passion for leadership drive the group they lead to fulfilment of their own ends instead of the group's needs.[23] Politically, Africa has suffered a lot economically, organizationally, socially and spiritually. Many times such leaders are self-centred and hate the good. In the church, such leaders fail to recognize and appreciate the giftedness and diversity in it that it was for collective blessings and achievement rather than personal ends. In fact, there is no gift that is superior to the other. All God given-gifts are for the benefit of the entire church, the body of Christ. Therefore, all gifts are essential for church growth; financially, spiritually, socially and numerically.

As much as leadership style is important for the church to consider in Africa, it should not be assumed that it is the only best. In the late twentieth century, politics of Africa turned to democratic continuum from autocratic. This also affected the church leadership in Africa. Although democratic style is not the best leadership style, it is the most heralded style of leadership for both the church and government institutions

23. Gangel, *So You Want to be a Leader!*

both in Africa and the West. It does not use the full potential of church human resources and expertise in terms of spiritual giftedness and the fruit of the spirit. Some people are elected into office not necessarily because they have a particular spiritual leadership gift, but because they have the favour of many people. The rule that works here is, "*majority must rule.*" It is not always true that majority has the best idea. However, it gives room to use other people's potential and expertise if the elected leader has wisdom to consult and respect the views of other people in the organization. The African church leader can use the potential in other people if s/he delegates other members of the church according to their areas of expertise, spiritual gifting and the fruit of the Spirit. "They allow an organization to leverage the knowledge and expertise of others to promote organizational learning and development."[24]

Sometimes church structures become church strictures in terms of use of church human resources. Some people elected into offices might lack certain expertise. And these are not the only people in the church. It is also impossible that all people in the church can take available positions since they are limited in number. Some people who might be left out in the election may have the expertise that might be needed significantly for church and social activities in the society. It is in this situation that people feel that they were elected because they were considered the best. As a result, they do not consult with people who are not in positions but have the needed expertise for some major decisions of the church and the society. My opinion is that this should change.

The church is the richest organization on earth. It has all the human resources needed to develop machinery or systems that cannot collapse just anyhow. Effective managers of the corporate world are members of Christian churches in Africa that are struggling with administrative issues. Why does the church perform so badly in its endeavours? After all, the efficient and effective managers are church elders or members of the church that is said to be the failure! Well, there might be reasons for that failure. One of the reasons may be African church's worldview of the secular or corporate world administration or management. If the African church's perception of the corporate world can be that all from the secular are evil, likely, such resources cannot be tapped. Second reason may be if the leaders of the corporate world who are Christians

24. Martz, *Leadership Development Architecture*, 74.

view people in the church as souls and think that they cannot use their skills for God ultimately, church's work may be passively done. All these approaches are detrimental to anticipated African Christian leadership development; particularly in the twenty-first century missionary endeavour. "When we realise that God has placed us in our job to co-labour with Him, contributing to His creation, it leads to a sense of dignity and destiny in our work."[25] In the twenty-first century missionary approach, there is a need for the participation of the whole African church in the whole mission. People with various leadership skills and expertise are what God wants to use in this century to finish the task of the Great Commission to the nations. Leadership is dynamic and corporate function of the church.

There is disparity in the exercise of power and authority in the church and the corporate world. In the corporate world, the position one occupies in the organization and its structure vests power and authority on him or her. The issue of servanthood does not count much in corporate world, unless someone is a Christian and would want to demonstrate his/her Christ-likeness character. In most cases, the corporate world is profit oriented rather than people oriented with exception of a few organizations that are non profit making.

The power and authority of the Christian leadership come from the owner of the harvest, the Chief leader, Jesus Christ. Christian leaders in the church serve as servants, stewards and harvesters. This is how our Lord Jesus Christ demonstrated for us to imitate. Power and authority are not motivating factors of Christian leadership. What motivates Christian leadership is love, ministry challenges and servant hood because these are the attitudes Jesus taught the church to demonstrate and are worthy emulation by Christian leadership in Africa.

The power and authority given to Christian leadership are for ministry rather than position one occupies in the church or the society. It is not for a leader to boss over people s/he leads. Of course we understand that a leader needs to make controls and enforce some decisions for the smooth running of the organization but the use of power should highly be controlled by the Christian attitude. The believers understand that Jesus Christ called them to ministry not to demonstrate their powers and authority over the flock they lead. "The church of Jesus must be

---

25. Hammond, *Biblical Principles for Africa*, 55.

committed to a lifestyle that is a reflection of Jesus Himself."[26] African Christian leaders must go a mile further in understanding what Jesus would do with the people they lead. The way Jesus demonstrated His powers and authority over demons, diseases, and other natural forces is how Christians ought to perform their leadership roles in exercising power and authority. We also ought to realize that Jesus Christ was both a leader and a manager of his team of disciples; therefore, he exercised power and authority. What and how did Jesus do? He served people and never lord them. However, leaders should play their leadership roles in a way that followers can take responsibilities over the flock they lead and feel that they are part of the church organization and leaders who care.

THE IMPORTANCE OF CHRISTIAN LEADERSHIP IN THE CHURCH AND SOCIETY

Understanding ones cultural and training bias on Christian leadership is crucial in the church as an entity of God. The church exists for God and His people. Christian leaders are not owners of the flock they lead, but mere servants of God's flock and they are responsible to Him for the flock's welfare. Servant leadership means leading the flock of God as a servant. In fact, s/he is also a sheep under the Chief Shepherd, the Lord Jesus Christ. Therefore, it is significant to recognize the importance of both positions of a leader as well as a sheep in Christian leadership. There is no disparity in importance of both of these positions in the church as well as in the society. In Christianity, leadership is a privilege. And as such, Christian leaders ought to be men and women of humility. God calls and gives some a privilege to lead his flock. In fact, he selects from the same flock those he designates to be leaders with leadership privileges. Christian leaders are just a step ahead of the flock they lead because God wants to communicate with his flock through leadership. He gives direction of activities of his flock to the leader to avoid confusion and conflict of roles in a team. Christian leaders must develop team spirit. They must consider every person under their leadership of equal importance with them because they are both children of the same God; for God raises leaders and he also pulls down when their work becomes incompatible with his standards and will. Remember the case of Saul the son of Kish, Ahab, Absalom and so forth. Christian leaders are co-leaders together

26. Lindsell, *Relationships: Jesus Style*, 85.

with God. Hence, they should provide a model of Christ-likeness in character and attitude toward the flock. They should have passion for God and compassion for those who struggle to grow in the likeness of Christ. They should bandage the wounded and bring back the strayed sheep. They must provide guidance to the church community and the entire society. This is why Christian leaders are supposed to be impartial and non partisan in execution of their duties.

TYPICAL CHRISTIAN LEADERSHIP IMAGES

The Bible has explicitly cited four images to signify typical Christian leaders as God expects of them. The Christian leader is a harvester, shepherd, steward and servant to the flock. He ought to lead by example just as the Chief Shepherd, Jesus Christ did. Although He was God He became a servant and demonstrated all godliness and humility for us to emulate while in the flesh. "You call me Teacher and Lord, and rightly so, for that is what I am. Now that I your Teacher and Lord, have washed your feet, you also should wash one another's feet" (John 13:13–14). That was a test of humility for Christian leaders in the church and Para church organizations. This is a scenario Jesus expects of Christian leaders to conduct themselves before God and His flock. This is more than just occupying a position of authority in ministry. Actually, it is a reality of biblical image of servant hood. Christian leaders, who fail to understand Jesus' leadership model of servant hood and humility, seldom do realize their position in ministry and the potential to develop in others who follow them. Jesus expects Christian leaders to reproduce their kind in obedience and character of Christianity as they lead and develop others into leadership.

Africans can be made into potential Christian leaders if only those Christians in leadership can realize and demonstrate Jesus' example in developing the potential in other leaders without emphasizing their weaknesses. Many African leaders fail to develop emerging potential leaders because they emphasize on the weaknesses of the potential emerging leaders instead of appraising them. The church in Africa is challenged to raise leaders who can have passion for God and compassion for the lost. The apostle Paul as a Christian role model in leadership for Timothy said; "And the things you have heard me say in the presence of many witnesses entrust to reliable men who will also be qualified to teach others" (2 Tim. 2:2). To the church at Corinth Paul said, "Follow me as I follow Christ" (1 Cor. 11:1). Paul realizing that he ought to be an example to the flock he was shepherding, he urged his followers to follow him. This saying signifies how careful Paul had been to his apprentices when they ministered alongside with him. Billie Davis observes that leaders are motivated and motivate others.[27] The senior leaders of the church should motivate younger generation to aspire Christian leadership. Leadership position in the church should not be view as an end, but a means to an end. The ultimate end of Christian leadership is the reunion of a sinner with his/her master and God.

EVALUATING THE CALL
OF AFRICAN CHRISTIAN LEADERS INTO MINISTRY

Understanding the core reason for responding to God's Call to Christian leadership is quite significant in African cultural context. The church polity in African cultural setting is such that some leaders are elected democratically while others are appointed and yet others were born leaders because they belong to the royal family or popular leaders in the society. Many times these systems of recruiting and developing emerging potential Christian leaders do not critically scrutinize factors of spiritual gifting and the fruit of the spirit. God gave gifts in the church for effectiveness and efficiency of His church. It is important that the church should evaluate the effectiveness of democratic system of electing leaders for church responsibilities because sometimes the majority or popular view might not be the best in God's perception and purpose of the church. Righteousness, gentleness, peace, love, patience, truthfulness, honesty, and holiness is not measured by the tool of majority must rule or popularity. It is measured by the attitude and relationship a person has with God and other people. Though subjective this might be, when it means things of God 'majority must rule' principle do not really apply. Democratically elected leaders might not be the leaders the church needs for the prevailing leadership situation in the church. Every situation requires specific leadership skills to deal with the problem. Therefore it is important sometimes to elect *ad hoc* leaders according to the situation the church might be going through.

In Africa, age, popularity and tribe from which one comes do matter when recruiting Christian and political leaders. No matter how demo-

27. Davis, *People, Tasks & Goals: Studies in Christian Leadership*, 222.

cratic the church might be in electing its leaders, these factors prevail and affect church polity. In some cases these factors cause voter apathy. Therefore, consideration of God's call for Christian leadership is noteworthy. Christian leaders are not supposed to be elected in the tribal or age or popularity lines. These are non biblical qualifications for Christian leaders.

Christian leadership should be considered as a calling by leaders themselves and not just as fulfilment of duty and occupation of office. The sense of calling into ministry guides the Christian leader to servant or shepherd leadership. At that point, the Christian leader can recognize and appreciate other people as fellow servants, co-workers, people of God, yet he has been privileged to become their leader. *First*, God calls people into relationship with Him. This relationship brings about regeneration to the prospective Christian leaders. It is this relationship that the Spirit uses to develop Christian leadership skills in the potential emerging Christian leaders and elevate some into position of service rather than authority as is the case in the secular. Yet this calling requires full submission to God's authority on part of a Christian leader. The call to Christian leadership is God's determination for particular people He relates with and anoints them and sustains them for the work He has called them for.[28] *Second*, God calls a regenerate man into the ministry of leadership. It is important that Christian leaders in African context ought to understand the concept of a trustee. As long as Christian leaders stay within the parameters of their calling, cultural impress has no negative effect on their character as Christian leaders when they lead.

Culture has an impact on every one's life; whether a Christian or non Christian. As Africans, there are cultural beliefs, values and rituals people hold onto culturally; even when they are born again. Nevertheless, as Christians, some of such cultural values, beliefs and rituals must deliberately be waived in order to incorporate Christian values that matter most for Christian leadership development and calling. In summary, the following are basic Christian values and beliefs for a Christian leader:

- The new life in Christ is vital for servanthood leadership in the church and society at large. It acts like motivation for reaching out to the lost in the society with compassion. It is life that has to be kept holy. S/he leads people to find salvation in Jesus Christ.

---

28. Shawchuck, *Leading the Congregation*, 59–62.

- The inspired Word of God should be her/his guide for his/her leadership endeavours. As such, s/he is bound to serve with humility as a model after Jesus Christ. Harris Lee quotes Martin Luther as saying, "A Christian is the most dutiful servant of all and subject to everyone."[29]

- The lost humanity is the most precious treasure God wants to save through Christian leadership ministry. Lost people must be valuable to God as well as to the Christian leader. The priority of a Christian leader is to seek and save that which is lost (Luke 19:10).

- Excellence in serving the Lord by serving others both in spiritual and social development of humanity as the Lord would is a must. Excellence in God's work is not an option but a must. There should be no compromise on the standards of doing God's work.

- The church is the body of Christ. As such, when leading people in His church one should understand that Jesus died for the least of them. The Chief leader longs to see them saved.

CONCLUSIONS

In becoming a Christian leader, the expectation of the followers is that of being a model in Christian character and behaviour. However, to attain that level requires submission and commitment of the leader to the Chief Shepherd, the Lord Jesus Christ.

Understanding the role of the Holy Spirit in the life of a Christian leader is critical for effective church leadership ministry; for without which there can be no difference with the secular organizational leadership. A Christian leader should understand that s/he is a servant of the Most High God, therefore, should obey Him at all cost. He should also be a model to the people he is leading. He must value what has been entrusted to him by God who has called him into leadership ministry. As an African in Christianity, the challenge is to live a transformed life that demonstrates Christian leadership development. It is also imperative to develop such values as the significance of the inspired Word, and servant hood leadership in the fellow Christians who are following Christ.

Western and secular African political leadership development has failed to provide a better and workable model for Christian leadership

---

29. Lee, *Effective Church Leadership: A Practical Sourcebook*, 85.

development for African church. It is therefore, important to rethink and re-examine the role of African social and administrative structures in terms of democracy since African society is going through cultural and political evolution. Other factors that need critical consideration in terms of Christian leadership development in Africa are the values of servant-hood of Christian leadership, the mission of the church and systems of electing Christian leaders for the church and the society.

DISCUSSION QUESTIONS

- Discuss the Christian leadership development model that fits well in African culture.
- Is traditional African leadership a resemblance of Christian servant-leadership in any way?
- What strength is in African political leadership for Christian leadership development for the contemporary society and the church?

11

Effective Pastoral Counseling Models for the African Community

- Introduction
- The Scope of this Study
- Definition of an African Marriage
- Universal African Traditions: The Framework for Pastoral Counseling in Africa
- The Evaluation of the Impact of Universal African Traditions
- African Risk Behaviors and Vulnerability to HIV/AIDS pandemic
- The African Society and Counseling for Decision-Makings
- Conclusions
- Discussion Questions

INTRODUCTION

A CRITICAL STUDY OF African cultures is essential for developing effective pastoral counseling models for the African society. Africans just as any other people have unique approach to their religious, social and economic problems. In Africa, each ethnic group has its unique worldview from which it develops its diverse cultures, thinking patterns, behaviours and customs. However, there are universal African rituals and cultures that act as framework for studying the context of pastoral counseling in Africa.

The current pastoral counseling training in Africa is lacking the African cultural context to develop an African model of pastoral counseling because currently most of the instructional materials and instructors come from the West. It is significant therefore to contextualize instructional materials to the needs of African community. Hence, the need to study the universal African cultures in developing an African pastoral counseling models for counseling people with marital, socio-economic and spiritual problems including HIV/AIDS in African communities. This study critically examines African marriages, religious beliefs, values and customs as crucial aspects to developing effective pastoral counseling models for African communities.

Understanding the religious beliefs, values, rituals and cultural marriages in Africa is essential and basic to developing models of pastoral counseling in Africa. The African cultures have been taken for granted by many theological and psychosocial training institutions for pastoral counseling in Africa. Most Africans who have been exposed to classical western philosophy in their scholarship have a tendency to take African cultures and philosophy for granted.[1] No two cultures are the same and similar. Each culture is distinct from another. People who are the adherents of those cultures are also unique and distinct in their behaviour and thinking patterns. Hence, they need unique pastoral counseling approach.

Most of instructional materials in theological and social training institutions for pastoral and psychosocial counseling in Africa have Western cultural and contextual dominance. This is because they are written by people of western cultural orientation. These Western training materials though good when they are used by Africans they are not contextualized in terms of uniqueness of the African society. It is imperative therefore, to understand that replication of cultures without contextualization can create a communication barrier with the counselee in African context. This study recognizes religious beliefs, values, rituals, and marriages as universal cultural practices of African community that form the framework of cultural context of pastoral counseling model in Africa. However, these are examined in the light of the scriptures to determine the biblical approach for pastoral counseling in the African communities. It is important also to realize that there is syncretism in the contemporary African cultures that are a result of western cultural and social influence and cultural dynamism.

1. Makumba, *Introduction to African Philosophy*, 31.

First, Africans are a tribal and oral community. As a matter of fact oral communities favor face to face communication with each other. They communicate orally while discussing issues affecting their daily lives. Second, the personal presence is more important to tribal and oral communities than literature or phone calls in Africa. For example, if your relative has died in the village and you are working in town, sending a message of condolence through any means without your personal presence would be considered as negligence or pride by most traditional Africans; though this trend is also changing in modern African society. Interpersonal relationships among the Africans are considered more important than everywhere else.[2] However, it is important to recognize that the strength of tribal societies is their community bond, interpersonal relationships and the impact of face to face communication. Face to face personal communication is Africa's heritage and an instrument of oral communication for counseling people living with HIV/AIDS, marital and other socio-economic problems. Face to face communication is essential for ministering to the basic spiritual, social and economic needs of individual persons and the communities in Africa. This fact has been overlooked, neglected and taken for granted by the western training instructors in Africa, both in religious and social institutions. Africans live as a community and communicate orally as opposed to literature and individualistic life style of the Western communities. Almost every decision in Africa is made in consideration of its effect on the entire community. African tribal societies are characterized by their strong group orientation. When approaching Africans with pastoral counseling, the counselor should be aware of group consultative decision-making process and solidarity of the African society. Africans are a 'we' rather than 'I' people. Therefore, pastoral counselors in Africa need to recognize the impact and influence of the community life on the counselee when it comes to decision making and developing self-esteem. Decisions in Africa are not the input of an individual, but a community. However, this does not mean Africans do not make individual decisions. When a person makes a decision in Africa he/she considers first, how the community will react, be affected and then, how it will affect him or her personally. Developing interpersonal relationships and communicating

2. O'Donovan, *Biblical Christianity in Modern Africa*, 11.

with people of community harmony is easy if the counselor considers incarnating into their worldview of unity.

Generally, culture serves as an identity of the society. It also shows the value system and cognitive patterns of a particular society or an individual that determine their unique behaviour. Hence, the study of culture while developing pastoral counseling models in Africa is essential aspect. Culture affects the way people think, behave and develop their relationships and conduct their marriages and other traditional practices.

In Africa, most marriages are endogamous. People marry from their own tribes and clans. This enhances community bond and extended family relationships among Africans. Since the pastoral counselor also ministers to married people, it is significant to critically study marriages in African context in order to understand the need for pastoral counseling models in African marriages.

This study will describe and analyze marriages in African perspective, religious beliefs, effective pastoral principles, and evaluate the universal African beliefs in relation to pastoral counseling in Africa. Finally the study will suggest ways of enhancing the development of pastoral counseling models in Africa.

THE SCOPE OF THIS STUDY

This study endeavors to explore the African perspective and a way of administering counseling to Africans in an effective manner. Africans are culturally unique in communication. It is vitally important therefore to understand the African cultural worldview in order to be effective in pastoral counseling.

For this reason, this study will concentrate on understanding cultural and religious beliefs that are generally conceptualized in the African cultural worldview; such as, marriages, rituals, the expectations of the society of a pastor in African context, and etc. It will also analyze how Africans communicate important messages to provide a strategy for counseling.

DEFINITION OF AN AFRICAN MARRIAGE

"In the Zambian traditional society, a man marries a woman. A woman never marries a man."[3] The Zambian traditional definition of marriage

---

3. Chondoka, *Traditional Marriages in Zambia: A Study in Cultural History*, 13.

suffices for most African cultural marriage contexts. In very few cultures in African societies a woman marries a man. In Malawi, for example, among the *Yao* tribe, women marry men. In most cases in such societies, the marriage pattern is matrilineal and husbands follow their wives. In this community, a husband leaves his home and relatives and joins his wife in her village. He becomes part of the wife's family. In some cases, he is enthroned a village chief in the wife's village.

In the family laws of Malawi, customary marriage is defined as coming together of two families to approve and witness the wishes of the intended spouses who fulfilled the customary requirements for the formation of marriage through their marriage sponsors.[4] This statement implies that for a marriage to be recognized in Malawi, it must meet customary requirement. As observed in the study of an African marriage, customary requirements include payment of dowry, bride price and probably the approval of parents of the coming together of their son and daughter as married couple through marriage sponsors. For marriage to be recognized as a customary accepted marriage in most African societies, the couple must be declared publicly as husband and wife either by the pastor or any marriage officer recognized by government. In some countries, for example, Zambia and Malawi, Village Chiefs are also recognized as marriage officers for customary marriages.

In Africa, when divorce occurs it is usually a husband who divorces a wife. The one who marries another is responsible to divorce. Wives also propose divorce where the husband fails to fulfill his marital duties such as having sex with his wife for a prolonged period without genuine reason; such as, sickness. Irresponsibility of the husband to fend for the household is another reason for an African woman to seek for divorce from her husband; though this is difficult in Africa because most women are not yet breadwinners. Further, battering is another reason for women to seek divorce from their husbands. Battering is considered as an abuse for women and it always has physical effect on women. In addition, in African context a man is expected to fend for his wife and the entire household. He shoulders a responsibility of fathering an extended family community. In other words, the African traditions give a husband more powers and responsibilities over a wife; though this trend is diminishing in modern African societies due to gender rights, influ-

4. Chibwana, *Lecture Notes for Magistrates Course No.1: The Family Law*, 3.

ences of the contemporary social, economic and political world and so forth; but the trend of giving men more respect and responsibilities is still evident in some African societies: particularly in rural areas in Malawi and Zambia.

Currently, the economic development and labour liberalization has opened milliards job opportunities for women. Women are employed and promoted to positions of influence in public or private institutions. They do business and earn income just as men do. Nevertheless, even in the situation where a wife is employed, the man is still held responsible to fend for his wife and the family. In case of death of the husband, sharing of the real estate, people consider the estate of the deceased husband. There is nothing like the estate of a deceased wife. These facts simply imply that it is the man who marries a woman in Africa. Theoretical Base of Pastoral Counseling Model

The Theology of Pastoral Counselling

A pastor is a shepherd to the people s/he oversees in his congregation and the community. Fred Greve writes that the word pastor and shepherd are synonymous.[5] The word shepherd is used as a metaphor in the Old and New Testaments. The Bible provides that a shepherd should show the following characteristics among others that are unique to pastoral ministry for counseling:

- S/he must have passion for God.

- S/he must have compassion for the suffering, oppressed and the lost (Matt 9:35–37; John 10:11)

- S/he must be a trustworthy person. A trustee is a steward who is a custodian of the trust. Certainly, this characteristic illustrates a responsibility on the part of the pastor as a trustee and a counselor (1 Pet 5:1–5). The pastoral counselor is trusted with the dignity and confidentialities of a counselee.

- S/he should be a faithful person. Pastoral counseling requires integrity. The pastoral counselor should always speak truth and only truth that is biblical and matches with his or her character; so that the personality of the counselee is not jeopardized in the process.

The pastor as a responsible person both to God and the people s/he counsel ought to take his/her responsibility with courtesy. S/he provides a bib-

5. Greve, *Pastoral Counseling: A Study Guide*, 33.

lical model to the counselee as God expects his people to live and behave. Impartiality, accountability, confidentiality and transparency are some of the qualities a pastoral counselor ought to demonstrate to the community whether in Africa or anywhere else in the world.

The Biblical Models of Pastoral Counselling

God gave counsel (advice) to Adam not to eat from the tree of the knowledge of good and evil (Gen 2:17). He does the same with all people he calls to his work; he gives them counselling before they assume any responsibility over his people. He does it directly and sometimes indirectly. Moses received a counsel from God through his father-in-low (Exod 18:13–26).

It is also important to recognize that the word counsel or counselling in the Bible is translated advice, purpose (Heb 6:17, [RSV]) or help. It also means guidance. When Peter, the disciple of Jesus Christ had caught nothing throughout the night, Jesus gave them guidance (counsel) of doing it the other way (Luke 5:4–11). In Acts 6:1–7 the apostles gave counsel to the disciples on the social problem that arose among them. These are but a few of biblical models of Pastoral Counseling for our example.

The Perspectives of Pastoral Counselling (PPC)

The pastor is a key person to understand the peoples' spiritual, social and economic problems in the society. Africans as well as any other people have unique stance over issues affecting their spiritual, social and economic lives in their society. Many times this is because of cultural orientation to reality of their world. Africans are no exception to these distinctions. They need a person of a caring heart to guide them thoroughly through the situation challenging their reality of the world. The study of Women and Law in Southern Africa (WLSA) found that the church is the most visited institution for counseling for decision in Malawi.[6] A survey by Evangelical Association of Malawi (EAM) (2008) indicates that most depressed people find a relief when they visit a church than any entertainment place.[7] These studies show that pastors need to be on the lookout to helping more people through counseling in the twenty-first century.

6. WLSA, *In Search of Justice: Women and the Administration of Justice in Malawi*, 20–23.

7. The Nation Newspaper, December 2008.

Psychological Aspects of Pastoral Counseling

INDIVIDUAL PERSONALITY

Guidance is a form of counseling. People like to seek for guidance whenever they want to take a new challenge or decision; especially for a career, a spouse or marriage partner and so forth. Adolph Aleck (2006) defines guidance as a process of providing help that make people freely adjust to themselves, to other people and to changing circumstances.[8]

Although this is determined by the individual personality, what drives most people to seek guidance is the bleak of the future and the results if the decision is made unwisely. However, the role of personality traits in this is the uniqueness to distinguish and choose between the best and good alternatives that counseling provides.

Personality in psychology means self identification among other personalities. Each person is unique with unique recognized identities; such as personality traits, likes and dislikes temperament, attitudes and so forth. William Bruce notes that sometimes it is difficult to predict attitude, behavior and interest of a person because of the influences of environment surrounding a person.[9] In counseling, it is imperative for the counselor to evaluate objectively the situation surrounding a counselee while providing counseling. In Africa, the influence of a decision may be impacted positively or negatively by consultative process which is a result of communalism.

MOTIVATION AND DEFENSE MECHANISMS

Naturally, human beings are defensive when their egos are challenged. Pastoral Counseling is sometimes confrontational; depending on the issue that needs counseling. In Africa, confrontation is considered as negative approach to situation; hence, it faces resistance. This is because Africans are community-oriented and consultative in decision making. Consequently, when they are confronted they consider starting the process once again as strenuous and time consuming.

Whenever the counselor considers confrontation as the best approach to an African, it is imperative to consider motivating the counselee first. J. Stanley Gray asserts that in learning situation the need to

---

8. Aleck, *Educational Psychology*, 45.

9. Bruce, "Personality and Children's Adjustment Problems", 101.

solve the problem motivates people.[10] There is a principle to be learnt here. When a counselee approaches a pastor for counseling, she or he is already motivated to find a solution to the prevalent problem. She is ready to face the gravity of the problem and what it takes to solve a particular problem. Yet the counselee's behavior or attitude when a counselor wants to approach the problem with confrontation should not be taken for granted. Sometimes a counselee is motivated by the results that will be realized when the prevalent problem is solved. Thus, motivation and defense mechanisms can be used as approaches to counseling in African society as well as any other situation.

THE WHOLE PERSON

Theological dichotomy or trichotomy of body and soul or spirit, soul and body do not apply in the theory of holistic approach to human problems in counseling. Jesus Christ died for the human being not just a soul. Pastoral Counseling needs to approach a person as a whole. For example, if the issue precipitating or requiring counseling was caused by sin, the whole person is affected and infected; therefore, consideration cannot just be spiritual or soul. It is the whole person who needs healing or restoration. Warren Newberry holds that people should be perceived as humans not as souls.[11] This belief demonstrates that when approaching a counseling problem the counselor should look at the whole person and address the problem as if it affects the entire person; spirit, soul and body.

UNIVERSAL AFRICAN TRADITIONS: THE FRAMEWORK FOR PASTORAL COUNSELING IN AFRICA

Types of Marriages in Africa

Generally, monogamy, polygamy, and marriage by permanent cohabitation are practiced in most African societies. The *ngoni* and the *Swazis* are culturally required to marry multiple wives; especially the king is expected to be a polygamist. Having several wives among the *Swazis* is a symbol of honour and authority. At this point, it is also important to note that homosexuality is not common in Africa because of culturally

10. Gray, "Creative Thinking, Reasoning and Problem Solving", 548.

11. Newberry, "PowerPoint presentation" *Master of Arts: Cultural Anthropology Class notes.*

set morals and ethics. In response to homosexuality, Robert Mugabe, the president of the republic of Zimbabwe argued that a dog knows a beach and a rooster knows a hen; how a man cannot know a woman.[12] In the same vein Bingu wa Mutharika in response to gender based violence also argued that all male animals defend their female counterparts why should men be violent against women and girls.[13] Francis Schaefer also notes that homosexuality is not common in Europe compared to the records of the same in North America.[14] Homosexuality is considered as sin, moral degradation and unethical practice in most African societies. Henry Malunda and Mercy Mpinganjira recognize marriage as legal union between a man and a woman living as husband and wife. This definition implies heterosexuality of marriages not in Africa only; but the world at large. Naturally, God ordained that marriage must be heterosexual rather than homosexual; therefore, he created people as males and females (Gen 1:27–28; 2:18–25; Rom 1:24–27). Biblically, marriage is also meant for procreation; as such, it must be heterosexual. In Africa, marriage is expected to be heterosexual rather than homosexual because in Africa, children are expected in every marriage. The value of children in any family in Africa cannot be underestimated. They are a glory of the grandparents from both patrilineal and matrilineal descent. African traditions have respect for people of opposite gender for marriage. Yet this is another reason why homosexual marriages are not generally common and accepted in Africa.

Nevertheless, most Africans are monogamous in their marriages except those who are influenced by traditional religious beliefs and Islamic religion. African Muslims and African traditionalist religious people are polygamous. Nonetheless it should be understood that monogamous marital practice is not a sign of Christianity in most African societies; although Christianity has influenced monogamous marriages more than any other religion in Africa. Monogamous marriages in Africa are not indicators of Christian marriages. On the other hand, some unbelievers practice monogamous marriages influenced by financial status not to have multiple wives because they cannot sufficiently

---

12. Mugabe, "A Response Statement to Homosexual Marriages".

13. Mutharika, "A Response Staement to Gender based-violence".

14. Schaefer, *Sociology*, 342.

and financially support them because in Africa, men are supposed to fend for their wives and the entire household.

Permanent cohabitation is not considered as legal marriage in many African societies. Some governments have constitutionalized permanent cohabitation as legal marriage; for example, in Malawi, the Constitution of the Republic of Malawi, Section 22, and subsection 5 provides that permanent cohabitation and marriage by repute as types of marriages recognized by the legal system and the government.[15] There are many marriages in Africa among unbelievers, Christians, and even among some ministers of the gospel that have the background of cohabitation. Yet, cohabitation is not generally acceptable marriage relationship by both Christians and the African society. A.S Hornby defines cohabitation as a sexual relationship of a man and a woman without being married.[16] Probably the definition of cohabitation may be unacceptable practice of living together of a man and a woman as if they were a married couple. This is whether the persons concerned are affiliated with any religion, denomination or otherwise. Cohabitation is sanctioned in African society and it is described as immoral and unethical life style, particularly by the evangelical Christians in Africa.

However, because of peer pressure and poverty in most African cities which is an influence of social and economic development, many young men and women cohabit, especially in institutions of higher learning and urban communities. Most churches learn it as a spiritual shock. Providing counsel to such couples is becoming a challenge to the church in most cities; especially where cohabitation is legalized. In order to develop a practical strategy for sexual purity needs critical study of cultural context of the modern African society. The social-culture in modern Africa is syncretic. African culture has drastically changed over the years because of Western cultural influence through language, dressing, foods, technology and education. Therefore, to establish whether a particular marriage is a Christian marriage in Africa, especially in the urban societies is a great challenge and requires critical study. Nevertheless, the church and the society consider cohabitants as immorally married people. In this human

---

15. Parliament, "The Constitution of the Republic of Malawi", Section 22. This provision is based on the 1994 Republican Constitution of Malawi before 2006 Constitutional Review process that is not yet active.

16. Hornby, Oxford Dictionary, 213.

rights dispensation, this is a challenge to the operations of the church in pastoral counseling; both in Africa and anywhere in the world.

The *ngoni* tribes in Africa are culturally required to marry as many wives as they can. It is a cultural obligation for a *ngoni* chief to marry several wives as a symbol of honour and authority in the society. Because of the tradition of polygamy among the *ngoni* tribe in Africa, the pastoral counselor needs to consider his/her approach and implications of pastoral counseling in Africa. Due to the contemporary pressure from the inevitable consequences of polygamy, as Douglas Waruta and Hannah Kinoti, editors observe, people in the contemporary Africa seek counseling from their relatives.[17] In most cases, these relatives are not trained counselors. They depend on experience and age that they are old; and therefore experienced. The African Pastoral Counselor should therefore understand the background of counseling in the African society.

Most marriages in Africa are endogamous. This is because Africa is strongly a communal rather than an individualistic society. A communal society values relationships more than an individualistic society. Marital conflicts in the endogamous marriages are easily be arbitrated because the conflicting parties are usually have the same cultural worldview toward marriages. Although most African marriages are endogamous, conflicts are inevitable and they should not be underestimated. The pastoral counselor should understand and consider the common ground of the conflicting parties – common cultural worldview. This can help him or she to understand the root cause of the conflict and thereby find a solution that is suitable to their cultural expectations.

Marriage Patterns in Africa

In Africa, both patrilineal and matrilineal marriage patterns are practiced. Each marriage pattern has its merits and demerits. The current demerit of patrilineal marriage pattern is the increased rate of property grabbing (WLSA).[18] However, this does not mean matrilineal marriage pattern is immune to the property grabbing issue in Africa. There are cases now being unearthed showing that men have been chased from homes by their wives just because there is wealth in the home now. This

---

17. Waruta and Kinoti, "Pastoral Care in Africa Christianity: Challenging Essays in Pastoral Theology," 34.

18. WLSA, *In Search of Justice: Justice Administration in Malawi*, 23.

is common where women marry men. This is also considered as property grabbing by women or their relatives. This study has found that poverty and African cultural inheritance model perpetuate property grabbing habit among Africans.

In Africa, only male children are culturally considered legible heirs of inheritance. Female children's inheritance is considered to be with their husbands. Yet, inheritance in Africa follows patrilineal or matrilineal descent depending on marriage to one belongs; and next of kin that is also a relative from patrilineal or matrilineal descent. This simply means that women have no inheritance in African society; unless all children in that particular family are girls.

Religious Beliefs in Africa

Most Africans are monotheistic. Due to cultural diversity in Africa, God is known by various names depending on the language, culture and traditions. Yet, some Africans are animistic and practice syncretism in their traditional religions. Many scholars who have studied African religions have concluded that African religions are animistic and that Africans are polytheistic.[19] Some conclusions are a result of interpretation of African perception of God in Western cultures, languages and mind-set without critical understanding of African diversity of cultures, languages and systems of worship that are unique to African societies.

The concept of a Supreme Being is one of the Africa's oldest beliefs. The names ascribed to God precisely show the godly consciousness among many Africans. For example, *Lesa wa Mumulu*[20] (God who is in heaven), *Mulungu Wamphamvu zonse*[21] (God Almighty). Richard Gehman records the argument of John Mbiti and Joseph Mithiani who argue whether *Mulungu* is a personal God.[22] To begin with, *Mulungu* is Chichewa and Nyanja word for 'God' in Malawi; and the Nyanja speaking people of Eastern Zambia also call God by this same name *Mulungu*. *Mulungu* is a personal God. In Chichewa and Nyanja, *Mulungu* is the

19. Magesa, *African Religion: The Moral Traditions of Abundant Life*, 23.

20. Bemba language in Zambia. Bemba people have known God with the name *Lesa* from time immemorial.

21. Chichewa language in Malawi. God has been known by the name *Mulungu* ever since. Knowing God in this way is neither syncretism nor animism as some missionaries have postulated. It is just the name of God in another language and culture.

22. Gehman, *African Traditional Religion: In Biblical Perspective*, 55.

same Almighty God in English. Yet, there are other adjectives that are used in Chichewa and Nyanja to describe Him further as it was the case in the Jewish community; for example, *Jehovah Jireh* (Hebrew language) for God who provides, *Wamphamvu zonse* (Chichewa & Nyanja), *Wamumulu* (Bemba) in Zambia, *Wakudenga* (Shona) in Zimbabwe. In Africa, most people believe that children, food, rains are a gift from God who is known by different names according to language, culture, and tradition.

The African societies are tribal and oral. As such, they have strong group orientation with mutual responsibility and group decision-making process. Tribal and oral societies interact with each other more often and they communicate face to face through oral traditions and storytelling. However, it should also be understood that people from the same social class and age group in Africa worship together and interact more often with each other, rather than in the inter-age and gender groups.

In Africa, age and gender matter in developing interpersonal relationships, communication and interaction with people of opposite gender and age. In Africa, it is also believed that counselors are elderly men and women. This helps the counselor to organize and counsel people according to their age group and gender. Therefore, counseling should consider social class of people and age group in African setting. Social classes in Africa may mean grouping people into gender, age, education and acquisition of wealth; whether they are rich or poor. Elderly people cannot be counseled by young people even if the counselor is a well trained young pastor. This trend is losing ground in modern African society. Elderly people are also seeking counsel from young trained pastors, though the number of such elders is still insignificant. They also seek counsel from young pastors indirectly. Again people with different age group cannot be counseled in the same counseling session. There are social and generational gaps between the elderly and the young people in Africa that may hinder effective communication in pastoral counseling.

African Rituals

A traditional African observes rituals strictly in fear of ancestral curses on his/her life. It is generally believed among non Christian communities in Africa that any negligence in observance of rituals may bring curses in the family or upon an individual. Basically there are two forms of rituals observed in African societies:

A. Religious Rituals.

In Africa, worship is mainly ritualistic. People like dancing; clapping of hands, singing hymns and choruses without looking at any written piece. This is encouraged by oral traditions of most African societies. However, rituals are observed and practiced according to events. The events are either religious or cultural. Aylward Shorter believes that Africans adopted some religious rituals unconsciously from Europeans during colonization and missionary regime.[23] Yet, it is also imperative to recognize that Africans had religious rituals before colonization and the coming of missionaries to Africa. Africans were worshiping God in their traditional ways ritualistically. When missionaries and colonizers came to Africa, they found Africans already worshiping God in their African ways of worship. So, religious rituals were not necessarily adopted from Europeans during the time of colonization as Shorter puts it.

B. Cultural Rituals

In most Africa countries, particularly in the rural societies when a child is born, people celebrate. First, as Magesa asserts that conception and childbirth are understood as blessings from God and the ancestors.[24] The celebrations for both conception and childbirth in Africa have mixed response: religious and cultural.

In a typical non Christian African society, a husband and a wife do not have sexual relations from when a child is born to a minimum break of one year or two. The African belief in this is, if they do have sex before the minimum period set by the tradition, it is believed that the child may die. Yet, the real reason for the minimum period of temporary separation in case of childbirth is child spacing.

The elders do not counsel the young couples about the child spacing when they join hands in their matrimony because children in Africa are considered as part of the family's wealth. The minimum separation period for couples who have a child is an old cultural ritual in Africa. However,

---

23. Shorter, *African Culture: An Overview*, 23.

24. Magesa, *African Religion: The Moral Traditions of Abundant Life*, 23.

in many African societies, this ritual is dying because people are exposed to many other alternatives for child spacing.

THE EVALUATION OF THE IMPACT OF UNIVERSAL AFRICAN TRADITIONS

The impact of universal African traditions is enhancement of oral traditions from generation to generation. First, the rejection of homosexual and cohabitation marriages in Africa is common. Second, respect to masculine and feminine gender for marriages is universally accepted in the African society. Marriage in African perception is heterosexual rather than homosexual. Third, recognition of worship of God ritually is common African practice. Therefore, understanding universal traditions in Africa is basic for counseling an African. Since Africans are tribal and oral community, studying interpersonal relationships is essential. Oral societies' communication is face to face talk. Most Africans would prefer face to face to literature and phone calls. Personal presence of a person you are communicating with matter much in Africa than any other way of interaction. Africans value the eye contact with the person they communicate very much. For that reason, pastoral and psychosocial Counselors in Africa need to understand what personal contact means in Africa.

As in any other society, religion and culture are basic for worldview formation. Members of the society interpret their world based on their Supreme Being, value systems, and rituals. Reality is perceived in the lens of their God and how they relate with him and to one another.

Homosexuality in Africa is not considered as marriage. The perceived and conceived African morals and ethics are such that homosexuality cannot be easily accepted. Robert Gabriel Mugabe in response to gay or homosexual marriages in Zimbabwe said, "A dog knows a beach and a roaster a hen; why can't a man know a woman." This by itself clearly indicates the relationship the Africans have with their God and the respect of gender for marriage relationships. Even so, the non Christian Africans also reject homosexuality on the basis of its incompatibility with human nature for marriage. At the same time it is important to recognize that there are some African nations that have legalized homosexuality. Yet, the countries that have not legalized homosexuality have been influenced by Christianity; for instance, Zambia. Biblical teaching on marriage asserts that one of the major purposes of marriage is procreation. So, homosexuality is not African traditional marriage. African marriages are heterosexual because they espouse children in their marriages.

Cohabitation, though it is practiced by many people in most communities in Africa, including some practicing ministers of the gospel, it is never held as a legal Christian marriage despite constitutional provision in some countries. Cohabitation is both a theological and social issue affecting African community. The first question that still stands out for the church to address is how should people who are cohabiting and are members of the church or are ministers be dealt with? The second question is how the church's relationship with the government which has legalized cohabitation will be, yet cohabitation is not universally accepted as a legal marriage. The sociologist Richard Schaefer defines cohabitation as the practice of living together as a male-female couple without marrying.[25] The society itself does not morally and ethically accept cohabitation as legal marriage though some members of the society do practice it. Some have suggested that the governments which have legalized cohabitation have done so for the sake of children and sharing of the real estate in case of death of either the husband or a wife. For example, Malawian government has legalized cohabitation to deal with the problem of real estate and reduce the irresponsibility among the cohabitants.

Generally, society's worldview is conceptualized through religious beliefs. The concept of a Supreme Being who controls life's situations and interpretation of reality depends on the conceptualization of God in the society's worldview. When people practice rituals with their commitment means that that is how they perceive reality; and Africans are no exception.

AFRICAN RISK BEHAVIORS AND VULNERABILITY TO HIV/ AIDS PANDEMIC

Africans like any other people are vulnerable to contracting HIV/AIDS. Many Africans who are not Christians practice cohabitation and polygamous marriages. Cohabitants rarely seek counseling from competent counselors. Usually, they enter into marriages without any counseling at all. This behaviour is vulnerable and risky to contracting HIV/AIDS. The polygamists are likely transmitters of HIV to the innocent wife or

25. Schaefer, *Sociology*, 340.

husband. However, it is important to realize that the habit of polygamy in Africa was before the discovery of the HIV in the world.

The church and the pastoral counseling in Africa discourage polygamy and marriage by cohabitation. Biblically, cohabitation is immoral behaviour; hence, it is condemned. In African society, cohabitation is also condemned as immoral and unethical cultural practice; although it is practiced by most Africans. Jean Garland and Mike Blyth note that a pastor must always remember that s/he is a shepherd and not a judge.[26] Although a pastor does not need to judge people, yet s/he must teach people biblical accepted practices or morals to the society. Basically, the African society and the church do not condemn cohabitation for HIV/AIDS reasons alone. Rather it is because of its incompatibility with the culturally set ethics and Christian norms.

People whose marriage is arranged with the church have a chance to receive counseling that might reduce the risk of contracting HIV/AIDS. Many pastors are now aware of the dangers of marrying without HIV test before wedding. Another risking behaviour in Africa is prostitution as means of income generating activity for women and girls. It is a fact that there are family households that are headed by children. Some of the children who are heading families are girls. In cases where these children do not have a relative from the extended family to guide and support them; morally, spiritually and financially, the girl child is vulnerable to contracting HIV/AIDS through prostitution. A study by Ephraim Chirwa observes that the number of women breadwinners in most African countries is still insignificant.[27] This is yet another vulnerable group of people in Africa. The pastoral counselor or a psychosocial counselor providing counseling to these vulnerable groups in Africa needs to understand these factors and pay much attention to how these factors impact individual and community life of the African counselee; and then, provide a guidance and alternatives as may seem possible to the prevailing situation and vulnerable groups.

African cultural practices are done in highly confidential manner. Seldom do Africans divulge confidential information to people of opposite gender; particularly if the information is most likely to bring about discrimination. For example, gender disparity in Africa is quite high. In

26. Garland and Blyth, *AIDS is Real and It's in our Church*, 55.
27. Chirwa, *Gender and Performance of Micro and Small Enterprises in Malawi*, 2.

Africa, men and women do not disclose to each other secrets that are gender or HIV/AIDS related. Data generated through focus group discussion in Salima, Malawi, shows that men and women fear to disclose their HIV/AIDS status to their spouses because they assume that will be the end of their marriage. Another example is: witchcraft is still a myth how it is practiced in Africa because of confidentiality. Consequently, most Africans hide their HIV/AIDS status after testing when they are found positive. Sometimes they disclose their HIV status when the situation is helpless. Hence, to help those who are infected becomes difficult. It is therefore, imperative for the policy makers to understand African cultural environment for HIV/AIDS counseling.

In developing a model for counseling in African, pastors and psychosocial counselors need to understand and consider culturally risky behaviours of Africans. Africans need to be convinced that keeping risky activities in confidence is hazardous to personal healthy life and of the society. Cutting of tattoos as means of receiving traditional African medicines is another risky behaviour that HIV/AIDS spreads. There is still significant number of rural Africans who depend on traditional African medicines which are taken through cutting tattoos. Although some people may use different razor blades; yet poverty and unavailability of adequate razor blades may be a challenge to some people. They may resort to using one razor blade for two or more to beat the time, poverty and the interest of the medical traditionalist.

THE AFRICAN SOCIETY AND COUNSELING
FOR DECISION-MAKING

In Africa, decision-making is a consultative process. Africans are community-oriented people; they do not make most of decisions as individuals. They prefer consulting with those who would be affected by a particular decision. Generally, in Africa, a decision must have a concept of 'we' rather than 'I'. Nevertheless, this does not mean that Africans do not make individual and independent decisions. Individual people make decisions that are particularly effective to personal needs and preferences not of the society; such as, size of the house to build, number of children to have and etcetera. These decisions in Africa are taken after considering factors like size of the family members including the extended family relations to be accommodated in the house and resources available to particualr individuals.

The largest population of Africans is not exposed to individualistic western processes of decision-making and priorities. If they are asked to make decision immediately they find it difficult to do it without consultations.

Second, Africans are non-crisis oriented communities. Non-crisis oriented people are characterized by finding the solution to the problem when the problem occurs. Usually, they have no plan B, in case plan A fails. In fact, they do not anticipate failures. For example, most African countries are found in food shortage crisis. But if you analyze the situation prior to the crisis, one would see the crisis from far; then, stringent measures would have been taken before the crisis. On the contrary, the crisis oriented society see the potential problem before it actually takes place and they find a solution to the problem in advance. This is not the case with non-crisis oriented societies of the African community. Therefore, this serves as an indicator to the Pastoral Counselor in African society to be careful when she or he provides counseling for decision among Africans. He should be careful of crisis and non-crisis oriented thinking patterns and behaviours of the African society.

CONCLUSIONS

The ministers of the gospel should critically study the African societies before launching pastoral counseling. There are several factors that need consideration and understanding when counseling Africans; especially in the rural African communities. They have the concept of God and sin. Contextualization is significant in developing pastoral counseling models in Africa.

Africans are a tribal and oral society. Their mindset and worldview is communal. First, interpersonal relationships and talking to each other face to face are some of the most cherished core values of both the community and the individuals in Africa. Second, community identity through ethnicity, emphasis on extended families and holistic approach characterize an African culture. Third, Africans are also known for their diverse languages even within the same country. Fourth, Africans have respect for elderly people; especially in counseling the youth. This is one reason why in Africa counselors are elderly men and women. Elderly and young people cannot be counseled together in the same group, where group therapy is needed they have to be separated into different age groups. Therefore, the most probable pastoral counseling model that can fit African society may need to consider the following:

- *Developing Interpersonal Relationships.* The counselor ought to develop good interpersonal relationships with the counselees. Good interpersonal relationship can enhance opportunity to communicate effectively with the counselee in Africa. Although interpersonal relationship is not only for African context, Africans particularly value it for their community identity and holistic approach to life. Moreover, interpersonal relationships provide face to face interaction and communication with the counselee. Personal presence is of great value in African societies as far as relationship is concerned.

- *Self-Identity and Family Relations.* Counseling process works well if the counselee has self-identity. Self-identity boosts self-esteem that eventually provides a premise for decision-making in counseling. Africans usually feel bound and responsible to each other and work collaboratively as a family unit. A family is a unit in which an individual feels loved and accepted and has an identity in the society. Therefore, when counseling an African, it is essential that self-identity is appraised and that family ideals are upheld.

- *Diversity of Cultures, Languages and Counseling.* Language is basic for counseling any group or individual people. A counselor desiring to counsel Africans should be oriented on some local languages because not many Africans can effectively understand and converse in English, Portuguese or French. In fact, most Africans do know their primary local language, and at most one or two other African languages. So it is a requirement for a counselor to learn a local language of the people he/she wants to practice counseling effectively. Psychological counseling terminologies may not enhance effective communication between the counselor and the African counselee. They should be simplified and defined in the language of the counselee. Culture is another aspect that requires critical consideration in counseling Africans. People in Africa just as anywhere in the world are culturally bound. Therefore, they perceive counseling according to their cultural worldview.

- *Respect for Elderly People.* A counselor in Africa should be conscious of elderly mentality which dominates most Africans. Age in Africa also means experience and experience provides the basis for becoming a counselor. In an African view, a counselor is an elderly person not a young person. Younger people are always expected to receive counsel from the older generation. In African perspective, counselors do not necessarily need to be trained in counseling, but they need to be elderly men or women in the society who are trained through age and experience. Age and experience in the society qualifies an elderly person to be a counselor in Africa. In providing pastoral counseling in Africa, the modern counselor should consider these facts very seriously and never take them for granted.

- *Formal or Informal Counseling.* Counseling in an African setting is both formal and informal. Usually girls from many African cultures receive formal counseling from elderly women (*Bana cimbusa*) in Bemba, *Alangizi* in Chichewa. The *bana cimbusa* or *alangizi* usually advise young women about good morals of their society. They are given counsel in raising children cleanliness of their bodies, homes and respect to their husbands. In Africa this is also considered as counseling.

Boys are counseled informally except in the communities where both boys and girls receive counseling formally, either from their religious advisors or traditional leaders. Generally, Africans are not formal (in Western definition of the word formal) in most counseling settings. Formality has little effect on communication and counseling in African culture. In most cases, formality is required when one wants to meet with the Village Chief or at the funeral ceremony. What matters in Africa is the event! The basic question usually asked to find out what happened is: did it take place? Not what time, how or where. One would conduct business meetings under the tree without actually offending an African.

With reference to the discussion expressed in this paper, the theological training institutions should consider advising the trainers whose background is not African on how to approach the course. Pastoral counseling in Africa needs to consider contextualization of the Western developed materials for study in African setting. African cultural and religious beliefs also need critical study and evaluation so that a proper counsel is given to the person needing counseling in a particular lifestyle.

Family and community bond should be regarded as influencers of the decision made by the counselee in Africa. Therefore, the pastoral counselor should consider communal factors, religious beliefs, interpersonal relationships, oral and face to face communication, marriages, and elderly mentality of African societies as strength in ministering to people in Africa.

DISCUSSION QUESTIONS

- What is your cultural definition of marriage?
- Critique African cultural beliefs of marriage in the light of your culture.
- Discuss the impact of communalism on endogamous marriages in Africa.
- State things that a pastoral counselor should be aware of when launching his/her pastoral counseling with an African counselee.
- What advantage has African culture for effective pastoral counseling?

12

Cohabitation Marriages:
Biblical and Social Contemporary Perspectives

- Introduction
- Background
- The Scope of this Chapter
- Definitions of Key Institutions
- Literature Review: The Challenges of Cohabitation
- The Challenges of Cohabitation
- The Roles of Institutions on Cohabitation
- Conclusions
- Discussion Questions

INTRODUCTION

THE KEY ISSUES IN this chapter are the biblical and social perspectives of cohabitation in the contemporary society. Although cohabitation marriages have been in practice worldwide for centuries, biblically the practice is considered immoral and unethical. Socially, some people cohabit because the practice is legalized constitutionally by some governments; and to some extend it is an expression of freedom and human rights. Thus, it is considered legal marriage. Since cohabitation marriages have been in practice for a long period, it is critically important to study the evolution and impact of cohabitation marriages. Socially, cohabitation marriages have been influenced by several factors including human rights, economy and culture. This study argues that understanding the role of the church, government and the family in containing the impact of cohabitation marriages in the contemporary society is essential. Cohabitation is both a spiritual and social issue. For this reason, the study of relationship of the key players in addressing the issue is significant. The church, the government and the family are some of the key players and co-partners in institutional development; and in addressing the impact of spiritual and social issues including cohabitation.

Marriage by cohabitation is rampant in our society today as ever before. The studies by Professor Jeffry Larson indicate that marriages preceded by cohabitation have increased from 10 percent in 1974 to 56 percent in 1994 in the United States of America. The study further found that 60 percent of students in senior high schools prefer cohabitation before marriage.[1] Members of the society cohabit for several reasons. Some people consider cohabiting because following normal marriage arrangement is considered expensive financially; particularly in Africa, among the cultures who charge exorbitant bride price; for instance, the *ngoni* in northern Malawi. The British Government Law Commission chaired by Sir Terence Etherton developed a consultation paper, "Cohabitation: The Financial Consequences of Relationship Breakdown" that has generated over 250 responses and continues to excite widespread interest in the issue of financial consequences of cohabitation;[2] while others say that cohabitation is just as normal as any other marriage: Professor Larson argues that cohabitation does not provide satisfaction and stable marriages.[3] Yet still others contend that cohabitation is a modern way of getting married in less expensive way. Some people cohabit because of peer pressure in urban communities, colleges and schools. However, Dale Wetzel points out that cohabitation in many societies is enhanced "because the meaning of the family has been altered by individualistic social values."[4] But what are the position and the role of the church on social values of the cohabiting couples? Are they legally married since each person has the right to exercise his/her freedom and that some governments have enacted laws to legalize cohabitation?

The issue of cohabitation is not only social, cultural and economic; but also constitutional, political and theological. Some Republican constitutions recognize cohabitation as legal marriage if the cohabitants stay

1. Larson, "The Verdict on Cohabitation vs. Marriage", 9.

2. Etherton, "Law Commission: Making the Law Fit for a Modern Britain".

3. Larson, "The Verdict on Cohabitation vs. Marriage", 5.

4. Wetzel, "Meaning of Cohabitation, Consequence of Cohabitation, and Conclusion," 279.

together for more than two years or over. For example, Section 22, subsection 5 of the constitution of the Republic of Malawi (1994) provides that permanent cohabitation and marriage by repute as legal marriages. The Republican constitution of Zambia (1991) provides that if people of opposite gender stay together as if they were married for four years or over should be considered married. Bumpass, Sweet and

Cherlin observe that in some countries cohabitation is tolerated because it is expected to become marriage eventually.[5]

In this chapter, the author contends that cohabitation is not legal marriage in African society both biblically and sociologically. He defines and analyzes concepts related to cohabitation, discusses theological and socio-economic challenges and contemporary perspectives of cohabitation, outlines the roles of different social and religious institutions affected by the practice of cohabitation, and finally gives recommendations or suggestions of the way forward with cohabitation in the African society.

BACKGROUND

Cohabitation is not universally accepted and recognized as legal marriage in the Africa society; as it is also observed in North Dakota that a man and a woman who live together without being married are committing a sex crime.[6] North Dakota has a record of 23000 cohabitants out of the 642000 residents. Yet cohabitation exists in the African societies as well as marriage, whether legally constitutionalized or not. Some marriages in the African society today are mere cohabitations. Unfortunately, there is little research on this topic in African religious and social institutions; as a result, there is no assessment of its impact both on spiritual and social development of the society and individual citizens. Therefore, cohabitation becomes a problem, and difficult to deal with by the church when the government Constitution legalizes it. What is the position of the church on the persons who are cohabiting and are legalized by the supreme law of the land to be cohabiting? The Bible teaches that Christians ought to obey the government authorities because they are put in office by God (Rom 13:1–7). The government constitution is the supreme law of the land and every member of the society whether a Christian or not must obey it. Does the church expel the cohabiting persons for not complying with church and

5. Bumpass et al, "Cohabitation- Trends and Patterns, Reasons for Cohabitation", 23.

6. Associated Press (AP) *News*, January 18th, 2007.

biblical teachings about marriage? Suppose the cohabitants decide to take the church to court for infringing their constitutional rights, what is the rational position of the church? This study analyzes biblical and social issues of cohabitation to understand the illegality of cohabitation marriages biblically and in the perspective of the African society.

THE SCOPE OF THIS CHAPTER

The topic of cohabitation has been debated from different perspectives; legal, political, spiritual and cultural. This clearly implies that it is an interesting topic. Therefore, it is important to define the scope of this paper clearly. In order to keep the content to the limit of cohabitation as handled by this author, this paper will concentrate its focus on the following issues:

- The biblical perspective of cohabitation rather than legal. However, some legal issues will be touched only from legal layperson's perspective. The author will neither develop any law nor interpret it in any legal perspective.

- The social aspect of cohabitation is covered to relate issues with reality of the African society. Cohabitation is both a religious and social issue: just as a society is both a religious and social institution; thus, consideration of its impact from both perspectives is equally imperative.

- This paper does not define cohabitation in terms of French political systems. Yet, such a view has been highlightened in this chapter for those who may need to pursue it further. Hence, it is not the intention of this chapter to deal with the issues of political cohabitation in detail.

DEFINITIONS OF KEY INSTITUTIONS

The Church.

The church is an institution and a community established to represent God in the human society. God established it on sacred laws for the welfare of the society. The church ought to demonstrate and teach morals, ethics and love to the members of the society as it is required in the Bible. Howard Snyder recognizes the church as a community of believers specifically called to perform four ministries: *diakonia* (worship), *kerygma* (proclamation) of the gospel, *kainonia* (fellowship) and discipleship.[7] A well organized and disciplined society is expected to reflect on spiritually and socially acceptable morals, ethics and love for one another. However, the church is also defined as the body of Christ; this means that it is a body of believers in Christ Jesus (Col 1:18–24). This body identifies or recognizes moral and ethical standards that God laid down for marriage and any other intimate relationships in the society. Therefore, observation and obedience to the morally and spiritually acceptable ethics lead to unity and enhancement of social development of the society.

The church biblically teaches that marriage is a heterosexually ordained relationship for production of children (Gen 1:28). Therefore, both the church and the society do not sanction cohabitation as ethical and moral marriage.

Constitution

Generally, a constitution is a supreme law of the organization or institution. The constitution must clearly stipulate how the organization ought to be governed structurally and administratively. It is an authoritative document for enforcing powers, roles and policies of official positions in a particular organization.

A republican or democratic constitution is a supreme law of the land. Every nation is governed by a constitution. Major official powers, roles and positions are defined in the constitution. It guides the nation how and what that government is expected to run the affairs of the people of the land. In some African countries, constitutions have legalized cohabitation marriages; for example, the Republic of Malawi. A widely consulted and accepted constitution reduces unnecessary political, social and marital conflicts. Thus, it is imperative that governments should ensure wide consultation when reviewing the constitution and doing law reform.

The British Law Commission Annual Report submitted to Parliament discusses the property sharing deal of cohabitants in case of separation or death.[8] Whether in Europe or elsewhere in the world, sustainability of cohabitation marriages is unexpected as Tom Freier affirms that cohabitation is not positive for the family, and poses a special risk for women and

---

7. Snyder, *The Community of the King*, 146.
8. Bridge, "Property, Family and Trust Law", 15.

children.[9] Women and children are the most vulnerable when cohabitation relationships break apart. Usually, children are not consulted when
a decision for separation is made. Hence, the need to study the topic of
cohabitation is crucial. Marilyn Stowe laments that in the midst of separation, a cohabiting couple experiences the same emotional turmoil as a
married couple going through a divorce. Even so, there is little—if anything—that the law can do for them.[10]

Cohabitation

Richard Schaefer defines cohabitation as the practice of living together
as a male-female couple without marrying.[11] The Republican constitution of Malawi (1994) section 22, subsection 5 defines it as living together
permanently of male and female. A. S. Hornby defines cohabitation as
a sexual relationship of a man and a woman without being married.[12]
"Cohabitation is when people live together in an emotionally- and/or
physically-intimate relationship. The term is most frequently applied to
couples who are not married."[13] Research in Social Sciences suggests that
living together in form of cohabitation before the wedding is not a good
preparation for marriage, or to avoid divorce as some may suppose.[14]
Cohabitation falls short of proper preparation of the couples for spiritual,
moral and ethical quality marriage. This is because the cohabitation relationship is always considered a tentative plan to actual marriage as the
Catholic Bishops in the United States of America argue that on average,
marriage preceded by cohabitation is 46 percent more likely to end in
divorce.[15] All of these definitions about cohabitation explicitly denote that
cohabitation is not legal marriage although the Republican constitution
of Malawi recognizes permanent cohabitation and marriage by repute as
legal marriages.

9. Freier, "Social Science Research", 2.

10. Stowe, "Cohabitation and 'the Common Law—Marriage' myth".

11. Schaefer, *Sociology*, 548.

12. Hornby, *Dictionary*, 213.

13. Available on Wikipedia, free Encyclopedia.

14. Wetzel, "Lawmaker: Anti-cohabitation law wrong", 2.

15. Catholic Bishops, "Cohabitation" 398.

Cohabitation is unacceptable practice of living together of a man and a woman as if they were legally married couple. This is whether the persons concerned affiliate to any religion, denomination or otherwise.

Politically, however, cohabitation in government occurs in semi-presidential systems, such as France's system, when the President is from a different political party than the majority of the members of parliament. It occurs because such a system forces the president to name a premier that will be acceptable to the majority party within parliament.[16]

IMPACT OF COHABITATION RELATIONSHIP

First, God's ordained morals and ethics of marriage are devalued and weakened. Respect to spiritually and culturally accepted norms of the society are also violated. Second, the contemporary generation may consider the practice of cohabiting as normative; therefore, marriages may not sociologically be following the society's established procedures of getting married; thereby corrupting the morals of the society and spiritual relationship with God who ordained marriage as a holy institution. Third, separation of the cohabitants may ruin the future of both children and a woman involved in cohabitation. Fourth, if there is no specific law to settle the financial matters of the separating cohabitants, the decision of separation may cause big losses and stress to the separatists.

ADVANTAGES AND DISADVANTAGES OF COHABITATION

Cohabitation is cost effective in its initial stage. The cohabiting partners contribute almost nothing to its inception. They just agree on some modalities to join the relationship. The practice becomes less permanent as responsibilities come up just as it does in biblically, socially and morally accepted marriage relationships. When one partner fails to comply with the agreed rules or fails to cope up with the cohabitation lifestyle the relationship breaks up almost in the same simple way it started. It is at that time that cohabitation becomes expensive. Usually the remaining partner bears the consequences and responsibilities of the casualties. The person who feels the pains of the broken relationship of cohabitation begins consulting with people who were not consulted when the relationship was beginning; especially in African societies. In most African societies, the decision for

---

16. Political Cohabitation: Definition .

marriage is communal and consultative.[17] All family relations from both patrilineal and matrilineal descents are involved in marriage arrangements. African society is 'depended on' rather than 'independent of'.

Marriage

Charles Kraft defines marriage as the socially recognized partnership between a man and a woman by means of which new families are founded.[18] Biblically, marriage is God's ordained heterosexual relationship of one man and one woman. Therefore, marriage is never man's invention (Gen 1:27–28; 2:18, 24–25). Marriage must be based on universally accepted biblical morals and cultural marital principles accepted in a particular society. John Stott defines marriage as exclusively heterosexual covenant between one man and one woman, ordained and sealed by, precedes by a public leaving of parents, consummated in sexual union, issuing in a permanent mutually supportive partnership, and normally crowned by gift of children.[19] Henry Malunda and Mercy Mpinganjira recognize marriage as legal union between a man and a woman living as husband and wife. Further, they say that failure to meet the legal requirements in marriage relationship nullifies the relationship to be recognized as such.[20] If indeed marriage is a legal entity as assumed by Malunda and Mpinganjira, and ordained relationship by Stott, then, it is probable that it is morally and ethically accepted in every society. Then, all members of the society need to take the issues of morality and ethics seriously.

The argument of Malunda and Mpinganjira of legal requirements of marriage relationship in their definition of marriage is significant when we consider the issue of cohabitation. Cohabitation is not generally acceptable marriage relationship by both God and the African society. Usually cohabitation is not sanctioned by the society, rather by the cohabitants themselves. However, they engage it at their convinience.

Marriage is an institution for spiritual and social relationships between people of opposite gender. Naturally, God ordained that marriage must be heterosexual rather than homosexual; therefore, he created people males and females (Gen 1:27–28; 2:18–25; Rom 1:24–27). Naturally also

17. Phiri, "Introduction to Pastoral Counseling in African Society" 11.

18. Charles Kraft, *Anthropology for Christian Witness*, 299.

19. Stott, *Decisive Issues Facing Christians Today*, 258.

20. Malunda and Mpinganjira, *Social and Development Studies Book 3*, 129.

God meant marriage for procreation (Gen 1:28). This concept of marriage gives the couple a responsibility over the children God may bless the couples with. In Africa, marriage relationships go beyond the intimacy of the two who get married to the community of the extended family relations of both matrilineal and patrilineal descents. Dale Wetzel asserts that marriage is secure and legitimate union when children are involved.[21] John Vernon McGee notes that there are two universal and very important institutions in the world that God has given human family, one is marriage and the other is human government. When these institutions are broken, the society falls apart.[22]

Recently, civil societies and other human rights organizations have been debating on the issues of morals and ethics in South Africa.[23] Biblical morals and ethics are absolute. It is generally accepted that God is the truth. The morality of cohabitation falls short of both biblical and social standarsd in the African society. Marriage is morally and ethically accepted when it meets the norms of the society culturally and religiously. In most cases in Africa, the cultural norms followed in marriages are also biblically set standards of the society.

People debate whether the Bible provides valid standard of morals or ethics. First, the creator of marriage institution, God, created the marriage partners male and female; thus, marriage should be heterosexual rather than homosexual. Second, the provision of *lobola*[24] (bride price) as observed in other cultures in Africa and elsewhere in the world is considered as moral obligation in the society and the church. In most African countries, the *lobola* is received from the bridegroom for the wife. Chief Katumbi of Rumphi district in Malawi introduced *lobola* in Malawi from Tanzania in 1780.[25] In Jewish culture the bride price would be received from the bride (Gen 24:52–53). Third, the Bible recognizes the social aspects of marriage. In Genesis 2:18, 24–25, the Bible asserts that the two shall be one flesh and the man will leave his father and mother to join his wife and they shall become one flesh as declared by Adam (Gen 2:23–24).

---

21. Wetzel, "Consequences of Cohabitation and Conclusion", 1.

22. McGee, *Thru the Bible Commentary*, 13.

23. SABC TV, "Debate on biblical morals and ethics".

24. *Lobola* means bride price or dowry.

25. Chibwana, *Lobola and Family Laws of Malawi*, 5.

The Bible condemns sexual relationship with a woman or a man who is not ones wife or husband. The sexual relationship or practice with a woman who is not ones' wife is considered biblically as adultery or immorality (John 8: 3–11; 1 Cor 6:16–18). Any sexual affection outside marriage relationship is biblically considered immorality. Therefore, anyone involved in such practices is biblically condemned for the practice.

Marriage Sponsors

It is universally, legally and culturally accepted that every marriage must have marriage sponsors. Marriage sponsors are culturally and legally chosen representatives from both sides of the couples. Culturally, it is acceptable in most countries in Africa that the bride and the groom be given in marriage by their culturally and legally chosen marriage sponsors. Cohabitation marriages do not follow this marriage pattern. No one gives any of them into marriage.

In Africa, marriage sponsors are usually immediate family relatives of the people marrying. The main functions of marriage sponsors in Africa among others are:

- To arbitrate the marriage discussions between the groom and the bride side. This function is particularly important until the wedding day.

- To arrange for the wedding of their son and daughter.

- To give counsel to the newly wedded couple; that is culturally and spiritually fitting in the society, if they are Christian. If conflict breaks in the marriage that may require arbitration, they are called in to arbitrate the difference and resolve the matter if possible. In case, the arbitration fails they refer the matter either to the church or civil court.

- To provide a model to the newly wedded couple.

LITERATURE REVIEW: THE CHALLENGES OF COHABITATION

Cohabitation may significantly weaken the biblical and social standards of the institution of marriage in any society. Michael McManus confirms that, "As parents or people who have influence upon young people, we need to tell them that cohabitation will set them up for a failed marriage."[26] Neither has cohabitation worked in the West nor can it work here in Africa. Cohabitation is marriage in illusion. In fact, those who cohabit, first; they just want to avoid children born out of wedlock. Second, they want to avert cultural requirements of dowry or bride price. Third, they want cheap marriage arrangements which eventually become extremely expensive.

Many times the cohabiting couples do not care for the children in reverential manner expected of parents. Professor Larson points out that cohabitation creates disadvantages for individuals, couples and children.[27] This practice enhances female-headed families and responsibilities. In most African countries, such families do not sent their children to school because of economic challenges. A study by Ephraim Chirwa notes that most women in Africa are not yet breadwinners.[28] This is one reason for high rate of illiteracy and street kids in Africa. In some cases, a husband deserts his cohabiting wife and children and goes to marry another woman somewhere even without genuine reasons for leaving his cohabiting wife. Usually, he continues with the habit of cohabitation.

Although some governments have legalized cohabitation by constitutionalizing it, cohabitation may likely lead to child and women abuses and ruin marriage institution both spiritually and socially. In Malawi where the constitution has the provision for cohabitation marriages, traditional and church leaders have argued to repeal the section that legalizes cohabitation marriages through constitutional review process.[29] It is also important to recognize that since God ordained government and marriage as sacred institutions, they must be treated as such. Research done in North America early in the 21st century, reveals that cohabitation is more common among African American and American Indians than in other racial and ethnic groups.[30] In North America, the practice of cohabitation seems to be encouraged by dating. Some young couples who fail to control their sexual passions during dating end up cohabiting.

26. McManus, *Marriage Savers: Helping your Friends and Family Avoid Divorce*, 93.

27. Larson, "The Verdict on Cohabitation vs. Marriage" 6.

28. Chirwa, *Gender and Performance of Micro and Small Enterprises in Malawi*, 7.

29. Nation News Paper, April 19, 2006, "Repeal Cohabitation Marriages".

30. Fields and Casper, "America's Families and Living Arrangements," 537.

In addition, Schaefer notes that cohabitation is common in Europe because of the general sentiment that says, "Love, yes; marriage maybe."[31] Charles Kraft describes that marriage is validated by a legal ceremony presided over by a pastor or other legally qualified person. Those who live together without going through this cultural form are considered unmarried, whether or not they successfully carry out the functions of the marriage relationship over an extend period of time. Therefore, the church needs to take an objective stand against cohabitation despite its constitutional legality. This also implies that the church should actively participate in forums of constitutional matters; so that its contribution on matters of national interest can be recognized.

Marriage, apart from being a social institution of the couples, it is also a spiritual and religious entity. As such, it must be God ordained. It must base its foundation on biblical and religious principles such as:

One husband, one wife (Gen 2:18–24; 1 Cor 7:2). Husband and wife relationship is heterosexual and forever (Gen 1:27; 2:22–25; 5:2; Matt 19:6); though this is greatly challenged in most contemporary forums worldwide because of the legality of homosexuality, lesbianism and gay marriages. However, cohabitation is not talked about in homosexual marriages. Do homosexuals cohabit? Submitting to one another as unto the Lord (Eph 5:21–23). Love for one another (Eph 5:25).

THE CHALLENGES OF COHABITATION

Theological Challenge

The Bible provides the solid foundation of marriage in Christian context. God exclusively ordained marriage institution exclusively for a husband and a wife. First, it was not just ordained for convenience for Adam and Eve but for worship of God (Gen 1:27–28). Second, it was ordained for procreation (Gen 1:28). It was God's intention from the beginning to fill the earth with mankind. Therefore, sex in marriage ought to be honorary and a gift (Heb 13:4).

In cohabitation, the primary reason for marriage is basically sexual convenience and studying each other for future marriage. It should be understood that the reason for marriage is more than fulfillment of sexual desires and matters of conveniences. Marriage calls the couples to a re-

31. Schaefer, *Sociology*, 340.

sponsibility to found and raise a family in which the oracles and fear of God have to be taught. Linda J. Waite and Maggie Gallagher think that many people resort into cohabitation because it is relatively easy to overlook major responsibilities.[32] Married couples are expected to take major responsibilities in that relationship as required by God, the society and the government. Therefore, cohabitation has in itself a spiritual and social impairment and it may likely cause economic default in the society.

Social Challenge

The church besides being a spiritual institution, it is also a social community. People meet and share their beliefs, belongings, worship together and interrelate with each other in many ways (Acts 2:42–47; 4:32). When the church disciplines the couple that might be cohabiting, does that for several reasons. First, it does so to teach its adherents that it is a sacred institution. As such, members of the church community must demonstrate Christ-like characteristics. Second, the church disciplines its members who are cohabiting to demerit the practice of cohabitation. Consequently, members of the church as well as of the entire society learn to observe acceptable morals. Third, it heralds the next generation the basic teachings of marriage that is acceptable by God and the society.

Usually, when people are cohabiting, they feel discriminated, undignified and socially marginalized. In fact, the cohabiting couple loses some of its friends. The estrangement of cohabitation relationship with the church or the society may significantly affect its sustainability. Thus, marriage institution can adversely be deprived of its naturalness and honor in the society.

Africans like any other people are vulnerable to contracting HIV/AIDS. Many Africans who are not Christians practice cohabitation marriages. Cohabitants rarely seek counseling from competent counselors from the church or somewhere else. By and large they enter into marriages without any counseling at all. This behaviour is vulnerable to contracting HIV/AIDS. The other reason is that the cohabitants are less committed to each other and their relationship; therefore, they find no reason for seeking counseling for the betterment of their relationship and healthy. Cohabitants settle for less because of lack of commitment; as Larson

---

32. Waite and Gallagher, *The Case of Marriage: Why Married People are Happier, Healthier and Better off Financially,* 43.

declares that chances of commitment and permanence are better in marriage rather than in cohabitation.[33]

Economic Challenges

Economic development whether of a nation or an individual depends heavily on healthy relationship with one another, commitment and permanence. In this paper, it has been discussed that cohabitation has negative impact on the relationship with the society and the church. Many times families with poor relationship become defaulters of economic development resources. If these are the members of the church, the support of the church droops.

It is a general norm that the groom's family pays the bride's family, the bride price. The significance of the bride price is to stabilize the marriage and give it its social and religious value. Stable marriage is most likely to prosper economically and spiritually because the couples share responsibilities and work collaboratively toward common goals. Generally, cohabitation does not provide such stability and commitment. Second, very few cohabiting couples trust each other because of the foundation of their relationship. Marilyn Stowe observes an increasing number of cohabitants consulting with her office; especially those who have learned, to their great shock that they have no legal remedy and share following the breakdown of their cohabiting relationships.[34] As a result, it is hard for them to work collaboratively. This impaired relationship may drastically affect the economy of the cohabitants and the nation.

Third, in the event that one of the cohabitants due to social pressure decides to desert his or her partner, the remaining partner if they had a child or children may shoulder the responsibility of looking after the children alone. In most societies, such situations create economic hardships upon the remaining parent. Single parenting is economically difficult venture for many people from an average family; particularly in Africa.

33. Larson, "The Verdict on Cohabitation Vs Marriage" 2.
34. Stowe, "Cohabitation and the Common Law of Marriage Myths", 23.

THE ROLES OF INSTITUTIONS ON COHABITATION

The Role of the Church

The church is both spiritual and social institution. It provides spiritual and social resources to the society and its members. The role of the church on cohabitation manifests in many ways and cannot be underestimated such as:

- To liaise with the government through the established machinery and structures to consider or reconsider the decision of legalizing cohabitation through the constitution. It should provide spiritual and moral guidance to the government on the implication of such a law on the acceptable human ethics and morals of the society. Tom Freier believes that repealing anti-cohabitation law would mean that the state does not value marriage and the societal benefits it brings.[35] It is imperative, therefore, to recognize that permanent marriages may enhance social development of the nation more than less permanent and uncommitted cohabitations.

- To relegate the habit of cohabiting among its members. Cohabitation is an example of moral decay in our society and lack of acceptable spiritual and social ethics.

- To give counsel to the cohabitants so as to understand the biblical meaning and importance of marriage. Marriage must be acceptable by both the society and God. Generally, cohabitation falls short of such a blessing from both the society and God.

- To mobilize young adults in premarital counseling and seminars. They must be knowledgeable of what is expected of them when they want to marry.

- To educate parents and members of the society of how God views marriage relationship and its responsibility over children. God's ordination of marriage is crucial in determining what it ought to be. Commitment to each other in permanent marriage relationship helps the marriage partners to develop plans for mutual prosperity and responsibility over God's provision of resources for the common good.

---

35. Frier, "Lawmaker: Anti-cohabitation Law Wrong", 3.

The Role of the Government

The government as an overall overseer of the whole society has a crucial role to play in arresting the habit of cohabitation. It should understand that cohabitation has negative impact on national development. Therefore, it has the following roles to play:

- To consult with the church and the society before enacting the law of legalizing cohabitation. The government must understand that it is God who establishes both a nation and marriages. Therefore, He must be honored by the decisions the government makes in relation to governance of national institutions and marriages in particular.

- To support or conduct thorough studies on the impact of cohabitation before legalizing it. Marriages officiated by the Church are universally accepted as models for the society. This is why most governments in the world agree with the standards set by the church on marriages. In marriage institution, the government and the church are partners. Hence, they ought to work collaboratively through consultancies.

- To set the age limit for persons to be considered for marriage. Generally, it is accepted that any one who is age eighteen years and above is an adult. As such, any one may marry at or after eighteen years of age. However, this also depends on the culture from which a particular person comes. Nevertheless, anyone below eighteen years of age is a child; therefore, cannot be considered for marriage.

- To educate the society on the importance of following proper marriage patterns in keeping with the church teachings about marriage and the universally accepted culture of the society on marriage.

It is the role of government to safeguard legally and culturally accepted marriages by providing laws that may avoid abuses of such institutions as marriage, children and women. Cohabitation is not an alternative to marriage. Kingsley Davis argues that if cohabitation were simply a variant of marriage then its increased prevalence vis-à-vis would lack significance.[36]

---

36. Davis, "Cohabitation: Trends and Patterns," 3.

The Role of a Family

The family as a sacred institution ordained by God to be a model of intimate relationships in the society has a very significant role to play in leading the society to the right direction. The family as a model of intimate relationship signifies the relationship Jesus Christ has with the church. In averting the situation of cohabitation, the family has the following role:

- To be a model of intimate marital relationship, demonstrating love for the children born and raised in that family. Members of the family constitute members of the society and the nation. Thus, well modeled family members may become good citizens of the nation and members of the church.

- To train children in the way of the Lord (Deut 6:1–3; Prov 22:6). The family is the first training institution for members of the church and any nation. Most unruly and troublesome members of the society are those who have not received adequate care and training in the home.

- To provide primary counseling to the citizens of the nation. Parents are divinely set at the basic stage of shaping up the nation for God. A good and admirable nation does not come in a silver platter; but from the full counsel of God through family participation in the process of counseling and modeling the future nation.

- To instruct the young adults in the family what marriage means. In African culture, talking issues of marriage with one's own children is considered a taboo; then, it is imperative to find someone to talk to children or send them to church for spiritual instructions.

CONCLUSIONS

Summary

Cohabitation is unsustainable and unbiblical type of marriage existing in almost every society in the world today. The implications of this marriage are detrimental to theological, social and economic development of the church and a nation. Divorce and desertion in the cohabitation marriages are common practices that have resulted into female or single parent-headed families. Female-headed family leadership hardly appreciates natural love experienced in husband headed family. In most cases, children born in cohabitation marriages do not have inheritance from their parents. In addition, it burdens some innocent people in the extended family with a responsibility of looking after children born in cohabitation marriages if the relationship breaks.

The church, the government and the family have diverse roles to play to ward off the situation. However, it is important to understand that the situation can effectively be done away if all the three institutions considered in this paper can collaborate in the work of de-campaigning cohabitation marriages.

Recommendations/Suggestions

Having considered the facts, evidences and analysis of the information in this presentation the author has come up with the following recommendations or suggestions:

- That the Church should consult with the government on legalizing cohabitation and provide a biblical and spiritual guidance on the matter; look at the benefits of both spiritual and social aspects of the society.

- Considering the negative and positive impact of cohabitation, it is advisable that the Church should take a biblical stand to believe that cohabitation is not biblically, spiritually and socially legal marriage. However, for those who are already cohabiting should be accepted in the church with an aim of teaching them the biblical perspective of marriage; and if they consent to the teachings they should be officially wedded.

- The Church should strengthen marriage and family institutions through biblical teachings. The family is basically an institution for a model of marriage relationship.

- The government should consider the negative effects and implications of cohabitation on the society and the future of the nation. A well governed nation depends on citizens that are well trained by their well organized families which cohabitation has failed to live up to. In addition, the government should rethink the role of good marriage in relation to human and social development.

- The government should consult with the church on matters that are spiritually, morally and socially integrated. It must understand that some people can take advantage of the weakness of the law to indulge in unacceptable, immoral and filthy relationships; thereby thwart the development plans of the government through developing poor relationships, desertion and failure to found and raise a family that can effectively participate in national development.

- Leaders in the families must recognize their responsibilities of raising members of their families in fear of the Lord by being an example to them and teaching them the truth about marriage. They must explain the implications of cohabitation and other unacceptable ways of getting married.

- That the co-existence of the church, family and the government was established by God for the good of all institutions considered in this paper in making a better society for the people.

- That more research be done on the impact of cohabitation on socio-economic life of the society in Africa.

DISCUSSION QUESTIONS

- Discuss the impact of cohabitation in your society.
- In your country, is cohabitation a legal marriage, why?
- Describe the position of the church on cohabitation as held in your country.
- In your opinion, should the government constitutionalize cohabitation as legal marriage? Why?

13

Divorce: Spiritual and Socio-Economic Impact

- Introduction
- The Analysis of African Marriage Relationships
- The Rationale of the Study
- The Spiritual Challenge of Divorce
- Divorce and Remarriage
- The Socio-Economic Challenge of Divorce
- Summary and Conclusions
- Discussion Questions

INTRODUCTION

MARRIAGE AND FAMILY ARE two inseparable institutions that God has created for both spiritual and social development of the society. The society is formed from the growth of marriages and families. Clans, tribes and nations are a result of the marriage and family growth. In fact, the economy and morals of any nation are the aftermaths of productivity of the family members. However, many people whether religious or secular do not really understand the basic reasons why God created such institutions as marriage, family, church, and civil government.

The critical study of the spiritual and socio-economic impact of divorce should bring out significance of marriage in the society. The increasing rate of suicides, orphans, poverty, illiteracy, as a result of divorce has inherently affected spiritual and socio-economic development of the society and individuals; particularly in Africa; and therefore, the negative impact of divorce cannot be underestimated.

John Vernon McGhee notes that there are two universal and very important institutions in the world that God has given to human family: one is marriage and the other is human government. When these institutions are broken, a society will fall apart.[1] Marriage and family are the most neglected institutions in the world. There is great concentration on organizing the human government politically and economically rather than family government which is primary institution to the human government.

There is little time and money spent on considering how the marriages and families are organized in our societies. When laws are made in parliament little efforts are made to consider how marriage and family affairs are run in the country. Many societies in the world today are chaotic because of poor marriage and family relationships. The supporting institutions for better marriage and family relationships are not strengthened and empowered. For example, the Ministry of Justice, Ministry of Health, Ministry of Social Welfare and Community Development, Ministry of Women, Gender and Child Welfare and the Church always have skimpy budgets to effectively support marriage and family institutions; especially in Africa. However, Ministries may differ according to the political structure of the country. Political will is basic to averting the impact of divorce through family policy development. Therefore, the study of marriage in relation to human and social development is significant, particularly in a multi-cultural setting we live in today.

This study assesses how the immoral responsibility of divorce can significantly affect spiritual development of the married couples. The other part of this study evaluates how divorce can haphazardly affect social and cultural development of the society.

THE ANALYSIS OF AFRICAN MARRIAGE RELATIONSHIPS

Family units form a society that determines the type of government that will be formed. If the society is disintegrated, it lacks understanding of core family values and biblical beliefs about the family because the family units are disorganized; then, the types of governments or organizations that will be formed may certainly be chaotic. Good relationships in marriage and families enhance well behaved citizenry. It is assumed that the most chaotic governments are a result of disintegrated family relation-

1. McGee, *Thru the Bible Commentary*, 13.

ships. Members of the society are expected to be taught good manners, marriage and family values and beliefs in the home. A well trained family member is likely to be productive in spiritual and social development of the society and the entire nation. It is important, therefore, to take interest in studying marriage affairs in relation to spiritual and social challenges affecting the individual and the society at large.

In Africa, new couples after the holy matrimony assume the responsibility of a parent or guardian even before they have their own children, probably because of extended family, poverty and HIV/AIDS-related death of parents. In African culture, the married couple immediately becomes an extended family and guardians of the orphans and relatives before they realize their own children. Adoption of children whether orphans or not in Africa is involuntary and informal, unlike in the western society. The extended family relationships in Africa culturally influence responsibilities of parenting on the newly wedded couple. Culturally, they are given either a girl or a boy to parent just on the wedding day to enforce the responsibility of a guardian or parent to a newly wedded couple.

The family unit constitutes the first government in any society. Father, mother, children and other dependants constitute the family government systems of every nation in the world. Good citizens learn to respect each other in their families before they respect leaders of human governments out there. So, in any society, organization or institution, marriage and family are institutions worthy consideration for development of efficient and effective national leadership.

God designed that children should be taught good morals and ethics right in the home (Deut 6:6–9). There is an English adage that goes, "Charity begins at home" (Anonymous). An organized and God fearing home is essential for raising obedient, patriotic and well-behaved citizens and leaders in Africa. Divorce devastates and deprives married couples and family members their peace, joy, and spiritual and social training for national development.

Each member in the family has a status, roles, rights and responsibilities in the family s/he belongs. When family members seriously observe and learn to take responsibility, exercise their status and rights at family level, the nature of the human government yet to be conceived is likely to be respected by all people. In fact, they are the very people who eventually take up positions of leadership in the human governments. Consequently in any society, divorce may be a big challenge to spiritual, economic and social development of the divorcees and the nation. The efforts of human governments to develop economically and socially are downplayed by mismanagement in families and marriages that divorce. Divorce, there-fore, is a significant problem worthy a critical study.

THE RATIONALE OF THE STUDY

This study argues that divorce has negative impact both on spiritual and socio-economic development of every nation, organization and the church. Divorced women and children are among the most vulnerable communities in our society today. A.G. Zulu writes that if a woman is divorced usually leaves husband's house with only her clothes.[2] This is usually common in African societies. A study by Earl and Moseley shows that rural poverty is deeper among female-headed households for a va-riety of reasons including the legal status of women, their social position and their participation in decision-making.[3] The divorcees are among the most vulnerable people to food insecurity, moral degradation and financial constraints in the society worldwide. Jiggins notes that about 30 percent of rural households in the world are headed by women; and the women contribute about 80 percent agriculture labour, they produce almost 60 percent of the food consumed by the rural population.[4] The participating percentage of women in socio-economic activities is quite significant to be considered by men who divorce. Seldom do women efforts recognized in social and spiritual development in African soci-ety. In modern Africa, women efforts for social and spiritual develop-ment are worthy recognition. A survey on causes of divorce in Malawi done in Zomba and Salima districts respectively in 2004 by Elishamma Ministries International showed that most divorce cases were a result of financial constraints and a great threat to marriage survival in most families that were surveyed.

The analysis of Jiggins and Elishamma Ministry's findings imply husband's ignorance of wives' contribution to family finances. Therefore, the impact of divorce is a great challenge to health families and national development. The challenges of the contemporary societies that might

2. Zulu, *Word and Content*, 28.

3. Earl and Moseley, "A Survey of Female-Headed Family" 4.

4. Jiggins, "How Poor Women Earn Income in Sub-Saharan Africa and What Works Against Them" 17.

be significant impact of divorce are HIV/AIDS spread, school dropout, poverty, stress, suicide cases, loss of status, and gender-related violence, particularly on the part of women and children. It is for this reason that this study is considered crucial.

THE SPIRITUAL CHALLENGES OF DIVORCE

God instituted marriage (Gen 2: 18–25). It is an institution for spiritual, social relationship and leadership development between people of opposite gender. Naturally, God ordained that marriage must be heterosexual rather than homosexual (Gen 1:27–28; 2:18–24; Rom 1: 24–27). *First*, it is realized that marriage is biblically established institution. Hence, it is expected that it should take after the morals and ethics that are biblical in perspective. *Second*, the issue of heterosexuality against homosexuality brings into conflict the interest of spirituality and sociological aspect of the society. In some countries homosexuality has been legalized constitutionally, while others are still contemplating and compromising with it because of religious moral issues accompanying it. Spiritually, homosexuality is considered unnatural, immoral and unethical practice; although human right organizations accept it. John Stott believes that those who cannot comply with God's standards about marriage have pervasive and integrated mind-set and he also notes;

> Marriage is exclusively heterosexual covenant between one man and one woman, ordained and sealed by God, preceded by a public leaving of parents, consummated in sexual union, issuing in a permanent mutually supportive partnership, and normally crowned by gift of children.[5]

Parents need to work in collaboration in parenting their children. Parenting children is a God given responsibility for both a husband and his wife. This means that each parent has a part to play in making life better for children both spiritually and socially in the family. The husband and his wife are expected to be the models to their children (Eph 5:25; 6:1–3; Col 3:21; 1 Tim 3:1–5). However, for some reasons the financial support may not necessarily be equally shared from both parents. In Africa, the percentage of working women is still insignificant; a study by Ephraim Chirwa notes that generally women have not been considered as bread-

5. Stott, *Decisive Issues Facing Christians Today,* 20, 262.

winners[6] and that they are marginalized in economic activities in some parts of the world. Nevertheless, mutual understanding of both parents of their responsibilities toward their support for children may have greater impact in the spiritual and social life of the children and community at large. The spiritual, moral, social and economic support of parents cannot be possible if there is divorce in the family. Divorce may bring financial, spiritual and moral challenges on the divorcees; especially children.

For the contemporary marriages to live up to high and respectful standards of sanctity, requires the couples and spouses to be fully obedient to God's word. Yet, misunderstandings and disagreements in marriages are inevitable; no matter how intimately their relationship or love might be. Marriage relationship always faces the challenges of living in dialogue, mutual understanding, and conforming into God's purpose and will for it and loving each other. Marriage is the only institution in the world where both the husband and the wife are invariably disciples of each other. God's desire in instituting marriage was that the husband and the wife would live in harmony forever. But to attain that harmony requires observation of two major biblical principles of marriage: submission and love from both the husband and the wife. This is God's command to the married couples (Eph 5: 22–28). To live in obedience to this command is a great challenge to both a husband and a wife. Therefore, misunderstandings and disagreements in marriage are obvious. Conflict in marriage is inevitable; what matters is how it is handled and arbtrated to the reconciliation of the parties involved. Certainly, gender-based violence is no excuse for such marital conflict and divorce. Any disagreements and misunderstandings between the couples should be settled considering the nature of relationship, love and God as the basis for marital solutions to such conflicts. Divorce is a disgrace to God and normal social life of the society.

DIVORCE AND REMARRIAGE

First, the term divorce and remarriage require definition. What is divorce and what is remarriage? Divorce may be defined as marriage dissolution while remarriage may be engaging in marital relationship of a person who was previously married or is separated from his/her previous marriage partner. Divorce and remarriage is a long standing unresolved issue especially among Christians. Josh McDowell and Bob

---

6. Chirwa, *Gender and Performance of Micro and Small Enterprises in Malawi*, 7.

Hostetler state that health professionals have concluded that separation of a child's daily life from one parent is more traumatic at some ages than at others.[7] Divorce and remarriage have caused some innocent siblings to face the spiritual and socio-economic challenges unexpectedly. Therefore, divorce and remarriage require serious consideration.

The exegesis of passages where Jesus Christ and the apostle Paul discuss issues of divorce and remarriage such as Matthew 19:4–6, Mark 10:11–12 and Romans 7:2–3, 1 Cor 7:10–13, 27, 39, it is clear that divorce and remarriage is unacceptable practice particularly for Christians. God did not permit divorce; probably that is why Jesus Christ in response to the question of the Pharisees and Sadducees on divorce certificate that Moses gave the people of Israel referred their case to Genesis 1:27–28; 2:18–25.

Most Christians believe that divorce and remarriage is allowed only where divorce is precipitated by adultery or divorce by unbelieving marriage partner and not otherwise. Jim Feeney points out those general statements in the scriptures that discuss divorce and remarriage that they require critical analysis on the sanctity of marriage and God inspired exceptions on the general rule for divorce and remarriage.[8]

Basically, it must be understood that when God ordained marriage He did not intend to abolish it at any other time. Marriage was intended for a life time. Oladokun (undated) argues that marriage is inseparable until death do us part. In many matrimonial vows the statement "until death do us part" is recited by the couples being wedded. But it is important to understand that when God instituted marriage, He intended it for eternity. Death came later as a result of sin. Marriage was instituted before man sinned against God. According to the sequence of biblical events, marriage was ordained in Genesis chapters 1 and 2, and sin came subsequently in Genesis chapter 3. Could have God predestined separation through death, since death came after the man's fall? Probably not, therefore, the issue of 'until death do us part' should be considered as a latter proposition after the fall of man. A statement by John Stott is worthy consideration here:

---

7. McDowell and Hostetler, *Handbook on Counseling Youth: A Comprehensive Guide for Equipping Youth Workers, Pastors, Teachers and Parents*, 201.

8. Feeney, "Divorce and Remarriage: Does God Permit It?" 17.

> Marital breakdown is always a tragedy. It contradicts God's will, frustrates His purpose, brings to husband and wife the acute pains of alienation, disillusion, recrimination and guilt, and precipitates in any children of the marriage a crisis of bewilderment, insecurity and often anger.[9]

The life of divorcees is an estrangement in the society. The spiritual and moral obligations of divorcees are infringed and impaired. As such, God's laws and purpose of marriage become devoid and meaningless. The people who have divorced are considered sinners before God and the Christian society. "What God has joined together let no man separate" (Matt. 19:6). In the cultural context of the Jewish nation, divorce was not permissible. When Jesus Christ was asked to clarify on the marital assertion made by Moses on matters of divorce, he said that God never authorized Moses to permit divorce. Nevertheless, people of Israel forced Moses to permit divorce. The contemporary society in Malawi allows divorce where violence is precipitated and life is threatened or endangered.[10]

Women were designed, created and given in to marriage to fulfill God's will and call. It is generally believed that God's purposes for marriage are threefold:

- For multiplication in order to fill the earth (Gen 1:27–28). Procreation is a primary purpose for heterosexual marriages the bible describes.

- For fellowship with God and with one another (Gen 1: 26; 2: 18–24). Marriage is a social institution for both spiritual and social development of the society.

- To help man fulfill God's call to the ministry of worship of God as a companion (Gen 1: 28; 2:18).

Man is created a social being. Being created so, his life makes no meaning without a companion. His or her life affects spiritual, economic and social development of oher individuals in the society where s/he lives. Marriage should be honorable in the community in which it exists. Respect of a husband and a wife in the society begins with how that particular marriage was arranged and officiated. If marriage is conducted in accordance

---

9. Stott, *Decisive Issues Facing Christians Today,* 259.

10. Common view in Malawi following gender-based violence, 2006.

with the spiritual and cultural expectations of the society, certainly it will survive sanctions from both the society and Christian community.

A woman is not just a helper, but a suitable companion of a man, her husband. Good News translation has the word 'companion' for 'helper' in New International Version. The word companion is significant in marriage relationship. In fact, the Bible says that God was not pleased when a man was alone in the Garden of Eden, and He said, "I will make him a companion" (Genesis 2:18 [GNB]). When man was alone, without a wife, God's purpose for multiplication, fulfillment of ministerial call and fellowship was dormant and meaningless. Hence, a woman was not created to help man multiply or fulfill ministerial call and fellowship only; rather she was created to be a companion even in bearing children. Therefore, marriage relationship is the union that helps both a husband and a wife do God's purpose and will in the world on one hand, and for national development of socio-economic development of the society on the other. It also gives both a husband and wife a responsibility to parent the children in the home; in Africa, this responsibility goes on to caring of the members of the extended family.

THE SOCIO-ECONOMIC CHALLENGES OF DIVORCE

Patrick Dixon points out that, "Life-changing faith was the real answer, people said. Then there would be no divorce, no poverty, no child neglect, no oppression, and no starvation."[11] Divorce in any society affects socio-economic life of the people parting and the closest relatives; especially children. In some cases, when the wealth accumulated is divided between two divorcing persons, it leaves both parties in dilemma financially. Each part does not get enough to live on. In African context, particularly when a woman is not employed, the situation is even worse socially and economically.

The most prevalent marital culture in Africa is matrilineal.[12] As such, when divorce has occurred, children and divorced woman become destitute and vulnerable to poverty, starvation and loss of status. Generally, whenever a person is financially incapacitated, s/he has no voice in the African society.

11. Dixon, *Out of the Ghetto and Into the City*,

12. UNAIDS, *Facing the Future Together: A Report of Secretary General's Task Force on Women, Girls and HIV/AIDS in Southern Africa*, 9.

In Africa, among the school dropouts and street kids, are the children whose parents have either divorced or they are orphans. In most cases, these children develop severe emotional stress, hatred and anger that grow against their parents and other relatives in the extended family due to insufficient parental care and guidance. It is generally believed that facilities of quality education and good healthy are the prerequisites for social and human development in any nation. Divorced children find it difficult to believe this phenomenon; because such facilities cannot be accessed. Divorce has contributed significantly to socio-economic downfall of many children and divorced women, especially those who are not educated enough to be employed in the African society. Therefore, it is important to find a solution to this problem as soon as possible. The church, the government and other partners in development need to mitigate in this human suffering; particularly in Africa. Probably, development of proper family policies would help in this area.

Psychologically, a person who has lost status in a society is incapable to participate effectively in development activities of the nation. S/he feels neglected and ineffective. Eventually, such feelings demoralize and affect efforts of social and economic development of the community and personal life. Generally, children who grow up with female-headed household due to divorce, because of insufficient learning, moral and healthy support and anger transferred from either the mother or father become very disorderly and odious. Some development studies have stated that children who grow up in scarcity of resources are likely to do better in school because they desire to catch up with those who have had adequate resources. Yet, the difference is so significant between those who have adequate and scarce resources; particularly those from the developing countries. The difference also depends on whether the children understudy live in the rural or urban, in a developed or developing country. "Poverty is strongly associated with social disintegration, marginalization, isolation and violence, and insecurity. No longer in development studies is it viewed only as economic deprivation, but also as an affront to human decency and dignity."[13] Seemingly, divorce is disintegration of marriage and other family relationships. Some other impacts of divorce are increased levels of illiteracy, HIV/AIDS spread and suicidal cases in the society. Some girls raised up in female-headed

13. Chilowa, *Bwalo: A Forum for Social Development*, 21.

household have resorted in prostitution because of lack of moral and financial support from responsible parents and guardians.

SUMMARY AND CONCLUSIONS

Divorce is both a spiritual and socio-economic problem. It impacts our society and community negatively, and the results of which are so enormous that they require multi-sectoral approach. Since divorce has indicated significant impact in the welfare of our society, the church, civil society, non-governmental organizations and government need to develop a multi-sectoral strategy to avert the problem. This study has pointed out that most pastors who train in Africa and in the West need to contextualize their pastoral counseling knowledge in order to minister effectively in Africa and among Africans.

Effective pastoral counseling model for African community requires understanding of universal African cultures and religions. Instructors of pastoral counseling in African theological institutions also need re-orientation of the organization of the African society culturally.

Pastoral and Psycho-social Counseling institutions need to be developed in Africa to deal with issues of marriage, HIV/AIDS and economic empowerment in African society. Counseling should aim at complimenting church efforts in social and human development.

Female-headed families need more attention because their socio-economic, spiritual and cultural problems are complex. A pastoral counselor in Africa should not take cultural, spiritual and economic issues in Africa for granted when providing counseling to African family members individually, and as a community. Therefore, the governments in Africa ought to develop clear policies for marriage and families.

DISCUSSION QUESTIONS

- What is marriage in your cultural context?
- Who is responsible for divorce in your traditional marriage?
- How can a church and government be of help in finding a solution to divorce problem?
- Discuss the spiritual, social and economic challenges of divorce in your society.
- Explain why in Africa homosexual marriage is not common.

14

Humanitarian Ministry and Missions in Africa

- Introduction
- The Theology of Humanitarian Ministry
- Biblical Model of Humanitarian Ministry
- Challenges of Christian Humanitarian Ministry
- Conclusions
- Discussion Questions

INTRODUCTION

HISTORY PROVIDES THAT THE Church was the first to provide social facilities in Africa. The missionaries from Europe brought Education and Health facilities to Africa. They considered reading and writing as basic to Christian communication of the gospel. The reason for the provision of education was specifically to facilitate communication primarily between the missionaries and the natives. Then, schools provided communication between the natives and God through the reading of the Scripture for themselves.

Although the first missionaries to Africa did not study the culture in Africa in order to understand why Africans behaved differently from European, yet schools helped to communicate the gospel. However, people in Africa got the gospel through the provision of education and health facilities. Not only did the missionaries bring the gospel to Africa, but also partnership in development with African governments in social and human development. In this chapter, the author will develop the theology of humanitarian ministry, biblical models of humanitarian ministry and the challenges of humanitarian ministry.

THE THEOLOGY OF HUMANITARIAN MINISTRY

Is the humanitarian ministry inclusive in the Great Commission? Should genuine believers be engaged in humanitarian ministry to the people in our contemporary society? Or should humanitarian ministry be left to the non-governmental organizations (NGOs) and the political governments?

There are various views pertaining to the ministry to the people who are in spiritual and social needs in our societies today. Some support the view that says, humanitarian ministry is for nongovernmental organizations; while others believe that humanitarian ministry is for the church as well. Yet others assert that it is for both the church in one hand and the government and non-governmental organizations on the other. But what does the Bible say in this struggle? For those who support humanitarian ministry to be taken up by the church, do they have biblical support of their view? Was there any such ministry in the Bible days? Does the Bible have such records of humanitarian ministry?

First, let us define humanitarian ministry. What is humanitarian ministry? The word humanitarian comes from the word human which stands for a being created in God's image. It is a being that has a body, spirit and a soul. Each of these components of a human being has needs. Therefore humanitarian ministry means caring for human beings spiritually, socially, politically and economically.

Does God really care for human beings spiritually, socially, economically and physically? I believe he does. Jesus Christ taught about caring for one another in the parable of the Good Samaritan (Luke 10:25–37). He has called believers to humanitarian ministry because they have ability and potential to perform better in this ministry (Acts 2:44–47; 4:32–35; 6:1–7), he cares for humanity and so forth. Terry, et al develops four principles to be followed in performing humanitarian ministry and the fifth has been added because of its importance in Christian humanitarian ministry delivery.

- *Incarnational Principle.*[1] With this principle, the gospel should not only be spoken but lived. The missionary should live the talk. S/he should be able to respect the traditions of the respondent society. Yet s/he should not compromise with the sins and laziness of the

---

1. Terry et al, *Missiology: An Introduction to the Foundations, History, and Strategies of World Missions,* 515.

respondent society. In all that is done in the individual or the society physically should appeal to the need of a Savior, Jesus Christ. Love of Christ should abound and be a motivation for daily humanitarian ministry to the needy; spiritually, socially and physically.

Humanitarian ministry should not be humanistic in delivery. The minister involved in humanitarian ministry should see to it that Christ is at the center of the ministry and the locus of service delivery. Ministers of humanitarian ministry should have passion for God and compassion for the needy regardless of religious affiliation or social status of people in the society who need such ministry.

- *Inclusive Principle.*[2] The ministry to the needy should incorporate spiritual need of the society rather than concentrating on the physical or social needs only. The ultimate need of every person or society is Christ, the Savior. "People regardless of age, culture or language have the same basic needs which are spiritual, social, intellectual and physical" (Phiri 2007, 24). The approach to humanitarian ministry should always be holistic in nature and never neglect salvation for the humanitarian ministry beneficiaries.

- *Human Need Principle.*[3] The humanitarian ministry is meant to transform the individual or the society so that they can appreciate God's love through meeting their immediate and ultimate human needs. "People should feel the love of Jesus Christ not only in words; but in its practical sharing of it."[4] The minister/missionary should carefully do need assessment survey to understand what needs ought to be addressed by the initiative of humanitarian ministry of the church. People as humans have needs that can provide an opportunity for missions. "People should be perceived as humans not as souls."[5] As humans, people in any society have needs ranging from spiritual to physical. Humanitarian ministry of the church should address all society needs holistically while demonstrating God's love and care for the needy.

- *Holistic Principle.*[6] Salvation is not the only need people have although it is an ultimate need. Sometimes people are not saved be-

2. Ibid, 516.

3. Ibid, 516.

4. Dixon, *Out of the Ghetto and Into the City*, 24–25.

5. Newberry, "PowerPoint Presentation" *Master of Arts: Cultural Anthropology Class*".

6. Terry et al, *Missiology: An Introduction to the Foundations, History, and Strategies of the World Missions*, 516.

cause the Christian approach to the particular society is not holistic and strategic. Strategic approach addresses the society problem holistically. It studies the problem carefully and designs the program in a way that begins with the most immediate or primary problem before dealing with the salvation problem; though salvation is the most significant problem. In fact, salvation is the target of the whole humanitarian ministry from Christian perspective.

- *Empathetic Principle.* People who administer humanitarian aid to the needy ought to demonstrate empathy. Humanitarian ministry in Christian perspective should not be done in fulfilling duty but demonstrating the love of God to the needy. Jesus expressed empathy in his delivery of humanitarian service to the needy of his days rather than fulfilling duty. Hence, humanitarian ministry must take the pattern of Jesus' humanitarian ministry to the needy.

The purpose of humanitarian ministry in the church is behavioral transformation from worldliness to Christ-likeness. This is possible only when humanitarian ministry takes evangelistic approach in a holistic manner. The minister who is involved in humanitarian ministry should be aware that he is not taken up by circumstances and compromise the need for people to be saved. Jesus Christ is all that the world needs most; though this is not reflected in most humanitarian ministries particularly those done by non-governmental organizations.

The church seeks justice and welfare of the society and individuals when doing humanitarian ministry regardless of religious affiliation. John Stott believes that issues of human rights, social justice, relief, and etcetera are reflected in the teachings of Jesus Christ.[7] Therefore, the church is in a better position to address these and other issues of humanitarian in nature. Tetsunao Yamamori says, "Relief and development provides some of the most fruitful opportunities for conversions, especially in people groups that would be hard for traditional missionaries to penetrate."[8] Humanitarian ministry is not for addressing physical and social needs only; it is for evangelism and missions too. "For the Son of man came to seek and save that which was lost" (Luke 19:10). Jesus Christ healed people (Matt 9:35–36) from physical, emotional and social sicknesses and oppressions.

7. Stott, *The Year 2000 AD*, 1–8.

8. Yamamori, *Penetrating Missions' Final Frontier: New strategy for Unreached Peoples*, 25.

BIBLICAL MODEL OF HUMANITARIAN MINISTRY

The Bible provides a model for humanitarian ministry. "Learn to do right! Seek justice, encourage the oppressed. Defend the cause of the fatherless, plead the case of the window" (Isa 1:17). Providing for the needy in the society is not necessarily a responsibility of the government or non-governmental organizations only; but the church also. The participation of non-governmental organizations (NGOs) in humanitarian ministry has rendered some churches in Africa to a hands free responsibility. Yet things were not supposed to be so. The church should provide patronage to all participants in humanitarian ministry.

When people had no food Jesus provided it. He sought justice for the woman caught in adultery (John 8:1–11). Jesus did not compromise with the act of adultery by the woman, but the case lacked integrity and evidence from the accusers. They failed to justify themselves in the case when Jesus Christ challenged their holiness, righteousness and justice. Eventually, he rebuked the woman and told her to sin no more. Children were denied access to see Jesus for no justifiable reasons. He rebuked his disciples and any others who did this. Then he called children and made them an example of the people in the kingdom of God.

The apostles and the first members of the church in Jerusalem (Acts 6) ministered to one another in more a humanitarian ministry than otherwise. The ministry to one another in the church in Jerusalem was more than just hospitality. The Jews and the Gentiles were brought together in the fellowship of breaking of bread daily and sharing clothes. "All the believers were together and had everything in common. Selling their possessions and goods, they gave to anyone as he had need" (Acts 2:44–45).

The Apostle Paul mobilized support from the churches of Macedonia and Corinth for the church in Jerusalem when there was famine in Jerusalem. This was like relief support for the people of God in Jerusalem (2 Cor 8 and 9). Therefore, the church needs to develop humanitarian ministry in order to meet all needs of the society.

CHALLENGES OF CHRISTIAN HUMANITARIAN MINISTRY

- *Compassionate Ministers.* Jesus Christ looked at people with compassion (Matt 9:36–37) and he mobilized workers and resources for the needy spiritually and physically. The workers in food distribution (Acts 6:1–2) were partial in their ministry to the needy. The apostles encouraged impartiality and suggested that servants in food distribution should be men full of the Spirit, wisdom and good reputation; while the apostles concentrate on teaching ministry.

It is one thing to mobilize workers for humanitarian ministry, and it is another thing to develop compassionate ministry workers. Many people who find their way in humanitarian ministries are not compassionate. They first alleviate their own poverty and other needs before the real needy people are ministered to. The apostle Paul taught the churches at Ephesus and Thessalonica that Christians ought to work with their hands in order to provide for the needy in their society (Eph 4:28; 1 Thess 4:11–12). Therefore, it is hectic for the church to develop and run humanitarian ministries without compassionate ministers.

- *Passionate Ministers.* Ministers in humanitarian ministry must have passion for God. Ministers who have passion for God certainly fulfill God's will in their execution of duties. Usually they are motivated by love for God and his people. They give their allegiance to God not by compulsion but willingness to serve voluntarily. Due to this, they stay away from corrupt practices that characterize non Christian humanitarian ministries. Passion for God is the drive for successful and impartial humanitarian ministry to the needy.

- *Training.* Training or developing people with passion for God and compassion for the lost is strenuous assignment. Training is one of the ministries that require a lot of resources. No organization has enough resources to engage into such a ministry. Hiring already trained personnel is expensive as well. Yet there is no better alternative but to train some for the humanitarian ministry if the church needs to succeed in developing the ministry as required biblically.

The theological institutions should include in their curricula courses that would prepare students to handle humanitarian ministry efficiently and effectively. Courses like economics, political science and theories of development and other social sciences should be contextualized to evangelistic requirement of the society.

- *Streamlining the Humanitarian Ministry and Networking.* Developing a theology of humanitarian ministry and mainstreaming it with other church ministries is a great challenge for many pastors and even for some theological institutional instructors. Humanitarian ministry should not be developed in isolation of other church ministries. In fact, the pastor ought to streamline all church ministries and network with other like ministries from other churches and organizations in the community where it operates.

Networking with other organizations may update the ministers in humanitarian ministries with the most recent information, problems and solutions. Humanitarian ministry does not need to cater for church members only, but the whole society. This is a challenge for the church particularly in the twenty-first century. The church may not have enough human and financial resources to meet all the needs for the society.

- *Resource Mobilization and Management.* To mobilize resources for church humanitarian ministry is quite hysterical. Economically, all resources are limited; and for the church to mobilize and develop already limited resources requires innovative pastoral team and membership.

The church is not a profit-making institution. Its resources depend on voluntary giving and sacrifices. Donation is unpredictable, hence, cannot be trusted. Yet networking relieves the burden of resource mobilization since the church can use the resources developed by other ministries or organizations. This is in terms of trained personnel, information development and communication facilities. However, care must be exercised in managing information developed by other organizations. Information and the personnel should not be abused in using them.

CONCLUSIONS

Humanitarian ministry must be theologically sound. People in the society look forward to receiving their needs holistically through the church; therefore, the church needs to understand society's needs holistically and provide for an answer. It is biblically taught that Christian should have compassion for one another and love for God in humanitarian ministry.

Humanitarian ministry of the church should be evangelistic in nature. Jesus Christ rebuked those people who followed him just for bread and fish (John 6:25–59). Humanitarian ministry of the church needs to go beyond providing food and clothes for the needy to providing the need of the soul and spirit.

DISCUSSION QUESTIONS

- Describe the Theology of Humanitarian Ministry.
- Discuss the Biblical Model of Humanitarian Ministry
- Explain four Principles of Christian Humanitarian Ministry.

Glossary

Absolute—Ideal, indisputable, and supreme statement; perhaps only God can issue such.

Adaptation—This is when you divorce the previous held view entirely and replace it with something new that makes sense.

Adoption—This is where you take in and practice the new idea or practice to be yours without completely divorcing the previous practice but rather modify it.

Anthropology—One of the human behavioral sciences discipline of study. It studies man holistically.

Belief—Anything a person or a society trusts and practices consciously or unconsciously as a matter of tradition.

Carnal—Corrupt or clever mind.

Catalyst—An initiator of something to happen or respond to.

Christian culture—A Bible based belief and value systems.

Church—A body of believers in Christ Jesus.

Community—Group of people identified with unique ideals, beliefs, values, character and culture.

Culture—A system of beliefs, values and rituals conceptualized into a worldview and practiced in a particular society.

Deity—A divine being venerated as a god.

Facilitator—A person, who acts like a catalyst to initiate some kind of training and thought process in the community.

Institution —An organization or a foundation established for a specific purpose.

Rational—An assertion based on reasoning.

Reality—An assertion that is certain or absolute to a particular society.

Respondent culture—A culture of the host community or society.

Ritual—Custom followed more consistently by a society or community.

Social Structure—A system in which a society is organized; either economically, politically, religiously etc.

Society—A group of people identified with the same culture, traditions and value systems.

Subtle—Doing things in a clever way.

Supraculture—A culture whose ideals, values and beliefs are above human capability.

Values—Standards usually set to guide a particular practice or vision.

Worldview—The way people or a person perceives things.

Bibliography

Adams, Jay E. A *Theology of Christian Counseling: More Than Redemption*. Grand Rapids, MN: Zondervan Publishing House, 1979.

Aleck, Adolph W. "Guidance: A New Dimension of Creative Teaching" in *Educational Psychology*, edited by Charles E. Skinner., 44–45. New Delhi, India: Prentice-Hall of India, 2006.

Associated Press (AP) *News*, "Anti-Cohabitation Law." No pages. Online: http://www .bookrags.com/news/lawmaker-anti-cohabitation-law-mood

Bakke, Ray. *The Urban Christian: Effective Ministry in Today's Urban World*. Downers Grove, ILL: Intervarsity Press, 1987.

Bellingham, Richard. *Corporate Culture Change*. Mumbai, India: Jaico Publishing House, 2003.

Bowling, John C. *Grace-Full Leadership: Understanding the Heart of a Christian Leader*. Kansas City, MI: Beacon Hill Press, 2000.

Bruce, William F. "A Teacher's theory of personality: Development, Dynamics, Ideal." in *Educational Psychology*, edited by Charles E. Skinner, 73–74 New Delhi, India: Prentice-Hall of India, 2006.

Bumpass, L. L., et al. 1991"The Role of Cohabitation in Declining Rates of Marriage." *Journal of Marriage and the Family* 53 (1991) 913–27.

Butrin, JoAnn. *Who will Cry for Me? : Pastoral Care for Persons with AIDS in Africa*. Nairobi, Kenya: East Africa School of Theology, Undated.

Catholic Bishops, "Cohabitation." No pages. Online: http://www.foryourmarriage.org /interior_template.asp?id=2039879.

Chibwana, E.D.A. *Family Law Lecture: Magistrates Course*.Blantyre, Malawi: Staff Development Institute, 1990.

Chilowa, Wycliffe. *Bwalo: A Forum for Social Development*. Zomba, Malawi: Centre for Social Research- University of Malawi, 1997.

Chirwa, Ephraim W. *Gender and Performance of Micro and Small Enterprises in Malawi: Working Paper No. 2005/03*. Zomba, Malawi: University of Malawi, Department of Economics, 2005.

Chondoka, Yizenge A. *Traditional Marriages in Zambia: A Study in Cultural History*. Ndola, Zambia: Mission Press, 1988.

Clement, Atchenemou, et al., *Cross-Cultural Christianity: A Text Book in Cross-Cultural Communication*. Jos, Nigeria: Baraka Press, 1989.

Clinton, J. Robert. *The Making of a Leader: Recognizing the Lessons and Stages of Leadership Development*. Colorado, CO: Navpress, 1988.

Covey, Stephen R. *Principle-Centred Leadership: The 7Habits of Highly Effective People*. New York, NY: Free Press, 1991.

Davis, Bellie. *People, Tasks & Goals: Studies in Christian Leadership*. Brussels Belgium: International Correspondence Institute, 1983.

Davis, Kingsley. "The Future of Marriage." In *Contemporary Marriage: Comparative Perspectives on a Changing Institution,* edited by K. Davis. New York: Russell Sage Foundation, 1985.

Dempster, Murry A, et al., *Called & Empowered: Global Missions in Pentecostal Perspective.* Peabody, MA: Hendrickson Publishing, Inc., 1999.

Dixon, Patrick. *Out of the Ghetto and Into the City: A Radical Call to Social Action.* Milton Keynes, England: Nelson World Ltd., 1995.

Elishamma Ministries International. *A Survey on the Causes of Divorce in Malawi.* Salima, Malawi: EMI Database, 2004.

Elliston, Edgar J. *Home Grown Leaders.* Pasadena, CA: William Carey Library, 1992.

Etherton, Terence. "Law Commission: Making the Law Fit for a Modern Britain." No pages. Online: http://www.lawcom.gov.uk/cohabitation.htm.

Evangelical Association of Malawi. *A Survey to Understand the Depression Problem in Malawi.* Lilongwe, Malawi: EAM Secretariat, 2008.

Fields, Jason and Lynne M. Casper. "America's Families and Living Arrangements." *Current Population Reports,* ser. p 20–537. Washington, DC: U.S. Government Printing Office, 2001.

Fotis, George W. *9 Most Powerful Ways to Improve Your People Skills.* Mumbai, India: Jaico Publishing House, 2006.

Freier, Tom. "Social Science Research." No pages. Online: http://www.bookrags.com/news/lawmaker-anti-cohabitation .

Gangel, Kenneth O. *So You Want to be a Leader!* Harrisburg, PA: Christian Publications Inc., 1973.

Garland, Jean and Mike, Blyth. *AIDS is Real and it's in our Church.* Plateau, Nigeria: Oasis International Ltd., 2005.

Gehman, Richard J. *African Traditional Religion: In Biblical Perspective.* Nairobi, Kenya: East African Educational Publishers, 2000.

Goodstein, Laurie. "Muslim Women Seeking a Place in the Mosque," in *New York Times, Monday*

January 26, 2009. No pages. Online: http://query.nytimes.com/gst/fullpage.html.

Government of Malawi. *The Constitution of the Republic of Malawi: Section 22, Subsection 5.* Lilongwe, Malawi: Malawi Parliament, 1994.

Gray, J. Stanley. "Creative Thinking, Reasoning and Problem Solving" in *Educational Psychology*, Edited by Charles E. Skinner, 548. New Delhi, India: Prentice-Hall of India, 2006.

Greve, Fred J. *Pastoral Counseling: A Study Guide.* Irvin, TX: ICI University Press, 1995.

Feeney, Jim. "Divorce and Remarriage: Does God Permit It?" No pages Online: http://www.jimfeeney.org.

Hall, Edward T. *The Silent Language.* Garden City, NY: Doubleday, 1973.

Hammond, Peter. *Biblical Principles for Africa.* Cape Town, South Africa: Christian Liberty Books, 2003.

Hesselgrave, David J. *Communicating Christ Cross-Culturally: An Introduction to Missionary Communication.* Grand Rapids, MI: Zondervan Publishing House, 1991.

Hiebert, Paul G. "Social Structure and Church Growth," In *Perspectives on the World Christian*

Movement: A Reader, 3rd ed, edited by Ralph C. Winter and Steven Hawthorne, 426. Pasadena, CA: William Carey Library, 1999.

———. *Anthropological Insights forMissionaries*. Grand Rapids, MI:Baker Book House, 2004.

Hornby, A. S. *Oxford Advanced Learner's Dictionary 6th Edition*. Oxford: University Press, 2000.

Ihonvbere, Julius O. *Economic Crisis, Civil Society & Democratization: The Case of Zambia*. Trenton, NJ: Africa World Press, Inc., 1996.

Jiggins, J."How Poor Women Earn Income in Sub-Saharan Africa and What Works Against Them", in *World Development, 17 (1)*, 953–63, 1989.

Johnstone, Patrick. *The Church is Bigger than You Think: The Unfinished Work of World Evangelization*. Pasadena, CA: William Carey Library, 1998.

Kietzman, Dale W. and William A. Smalley. "The Missionary's Role in Culture Change" In *Perspectives On the World Christian Movement: A Reader* 3rd Edition, eds. Ralph C. Winter and Stephen Hawthorne. Pasadena, CA: William Carey Library, 1978.

Kluckholn, Clyde. *Mirror for Man*. New York: Whittlesey, 1949.

Kraft, Charles H. "Culture, Worldview and Contextualization." In *Perspectives On the World Christian Movement: A Reader* 3rd Edition, eds. Ralph D. Winter and Steven C. Hawthorne, 385. Pasadena, CA: William Carey Library, 1999.

———. *Anthropology for Christian Witness*. Maryknoll, NY: Orbis Books, 2003.

Kraft, Marguerite G. *Understanding Spiritual Power: A Forgotten Dimension of Cross-Cultural Mission and Ministry*. Maryknoll, NY: Orbis Books, 1995.

Larson, Jeffry H. "The Verdict on Cohabitation vs. Marriage". No pages Online: http://marriageandfamilies.byu.edu/issues/2001/january/cohabitation.htm.

Latourette, Kenneth Scott. *A History of Christianity: Beginnings to 1500*. Volume I. Peabody, MA: Prince Press, 2003.

Lee, Harris W. *Effective Church Leadership: A Practical Sourcebook*. Silver Spring, MD: Ministerial Association General Conference of Seventh-Day Adventists, 2003.

Lenneiye, Mungai Nginya. *Quest for a Corporate African Leadership: Public Sector Case Studies from Southern Africa*. Harare, Zimbabwe: Nehanda Publishers Ltd, 2000.

Lindsell, Stuart. *Relationships: Jesus Style*. Milton Keynes, England: Word Publishing Books, 1992.

Lingenfelter, Sherwood G. and Marvin K. Mayers. *Ministering Cross-Culturally: An Incarnational Model for Personal Relationships*. Grand Rapids, MI: Baker Academic, 2005.

Luzbetak, Louis J. *The Church and Cultures: New Perspectives in Missiological Anthropology*. Maryknoll, NY: Orbis Books, 2000.

Lwaminda, Peter. "The Church as Family and the Quest for Justice and Peace in Africa" in *Inculturating the Church in Africa: Theological and Practical Perspectives*, Cecil McGarry and Patrick Ryan (eds). Nairobi, Kenya: Paulines Publications, 2001.

Lyons, Linda. "The Future of Marriage: Part II." *Gallop Poll Tuesday Briefing*, July 30, 2000.

Magesa, Laurenti. *African Religion: The Moral Traditions of Abundant Life*. Nairobi, Kemya: Paulines Publications Africa, 1997.

Makumba, Maurice M. *Introduction to African Philosophy*. Nairobi, Kenya: Paulines Publications, 2007.

Malunda, Henry and Mercy Mpinganjira. *Social and Development Studies Book 3*. Blantyre, Malawi: Jhango Heimann Publishing Co., undated.

Martz, David. *Leadership Development Architecture.*Springfield, MO: Life Publishers International, 2002.

Maxwell, John C. *The 17 Essential Qualities of a Team Player: Becoming the Kind of Person Every Team Wants*. Mumbai, India: Magna Publishing Co. Ltd., 2002.

McBride, Neal F. *How to Lead Small Groups*. Colorado Springs, CO: Navpress, 1990.

McDowell and Bob Hostetler. *Handbook on Counseling Youth: A Comprehensive Guide for Equipping Youth Workers, Pastors, Teachers and Parents*. Nashville, TE: W Publishing Group, 1996.

McGhee, John Vernon. *Thru The Bible Commentary Series: The Law of Genesis*. Nashville, TE: Thomas Nelson Publishers, 1991.

McIntosh, Gary L & Rima, Samuel D. *Overcoming the Dark Side of Leadership: The Paradox of Personal Dysfunction*. Grand Rapids, MN: Baker Book House Co., 1997.

McManus, Michael. *Marriage Savers: Helping Your Friend and Family Avoid Divorce*. Grand Rapids, MN: Zondervan Publishing House, 1995.

Megyery, Kathy, *Women in Canadian Politics: Toward Equity in Representation*. Editor, Vol.6. Research Studies, Toronto and Oxford: Dunturn Press, 1991.

Mhagama, Christian. "Pauline Churches as God's Family: A Search from the Roots" in *Inculturating the Church in Africa: Theological and Practical Perspectives*, Cecil McGarry and Patrick Ryan (eds). Nairobi, Kenya: Paulines Publications, 2001.

Ministry of Gender, Women and Child Welfare, *Gender Policy*. Lilongwe, Malawi: Malawi Government, 2003.

Mufune, Pempelani O. and Mwansa, Lengwe K. *Supervisory Women and Men in Work Organizations*. Gaborone, Botswana: M and M Ltd., 1993

Mugabe, Robert G. "A Response to Homosexual Marriages in Zimbabwe" Press Statement., Government of Zimbabwe, 2000.

Museveni, Y.K. *What is Africa's problem? Speeches and writings on Africa*. Kampala: NRM Publications, 1992.

Mutharika, Bingu Wa. "A Response to Gender-Based Violence" Press Statement. Government of Malawi, 2006.

Neil, James. "Analysis of Professional Literature." No pages. Online: http://www.wilderdom.com/OEcourses/PROFLIT/Class6Qualitative1.htm.

Neil, Stephen. *Jesus Through Many Eyes*. Philadelphia: Fortress, 1996.

Ngatia, Peter M. and Mutema, Alfred M. *Principles and Practices of Problem-Based Learning*. Nairobi, Kenya: Moi University Press, 2006.

Niemeyer, Larry. *Cultural Anthropology: Cultural Studies for Ministry Practitioners*. Springfield, MO: Global University Press, 2005.

O'Donovan, Wilbur. *Biblical Christianity in Modern Africa*. Waynesboro, GA: Paternoster Press, 2000.

Osei-Mensah, Gottfried. *Wanted: Servant Leaders Theological Perspectives in Africa*. Achimota, Ghana: Africa Christian Press, 1990.

Pembamoyo, Eston Dickson. "Religion: Democracy in the Church," *Weekend Nation 24–25 June* Blantyre, Malawi: Nation Publications, 2006.

Phiri, George Allan. "Women Empowerment for Missions: A Capacity Building Program for a Local Church" Master of Arts Capstone Project Paper, Global University, 2007.

———. *Biblical Principles of Teaching: A Study Guide for Teachers and Ministers*. Lilongwe, Malawi: Assemblies of God School of Theology, 2007.

———. *Cross-Cultural Communication: A Study Guide*. Lusaka, Zambia: Christian Vocation Training Center, 2008.

————. *Cultural Anthropology: A Study Guide.* Lusaka, Zambia: Christian Vocation Training Center, 2009.

Political Cohabitation: Oxford Dictionary Definition. No page Online:http://www .answers.com/topic/two-party-system.

Reed, Layman E. *Preparing Missionaries: For Intercultural Communication.* Pasadena, CA: William Carey Library, 1985.

Roberts, Randal. *Lessons in Leadership: Fifty Respected Evangelical Leaders Share Their Wisdom on Ministry.* Grand Rapids, MI: Kregel Publications, 1999.

Rommen, Edward., and Gary Corwin. *Missiology and the Social sciences: Contributions, Cautions and Conclusions.* Pasadena, CA: William Carey Library, 1996.

Ryan, Patrick M. "Building a New Idea and Image of Church" in *Inculturating the Church in Africa: Theological and Practical Perspectives,* eds. Cecil McGarry and Patrick Ryan Nairobi, Kenya: Paulines Publications Africa, 2001.

Schaefer, Richard T. *Sociology.* New York, NY: McGraw Hill Higher Education, 2005.

Schwarz, Christian A. *Natural Church Development: A Guide to Eight Essential Qualities of Healthy Churches.* Carol Stream, IL: ChurchSmart Resources, 1999.

Shawchuck, Norman and Heuser, Rogers. *Leading the Congregation.* Nahville, TN: Abingdon Press, 1993.

Shorter, Aylward. *African Culture: An Overview.* Nairobi, Kenya: Paulines Publications Africa, 1998.

Simons, Tavia and Martin O'Connell. "Married-Couple and Unmarried Partner Households: 2000."

Census 2000 Special Reports CENBR-5. Washington DC: U.S. Government Printing Office, 2003.

Sire, James W. *Scripture Twisting.* Downers Grove, IL: Intervarsity Press, 1980.

Smith, Fred Sr. *Leading With Integrity: Competence with Christian Character.* Minneapolis, MA: Bethany House Publishers, 1999.

Snyder, Howard. *Community of the King.* Grand Rapids, MN: Intervarsity Press, 1977.

South African Broadcasting Corporation (SABC) TV. "Debate on Morals and Ethics" quoted in April, 2008.

Stott, John. *The Year 2000 AD.* Basingstoke, Hants: Marshall Morgan & Scott, 1983.

————. *Decisive Issues Facing Christians Today.* Grand Rapids, MI: Baker Book House, 1984.

Stowe, Marilyn "Cohabitation and 'the Common Law Marriage' myth". No page Online: http://www.foryourmarriage.org/interior_template.asp?id=203989.

Stuart Bridge, "Property, Family and Trust Law". No page Online: http://www.lawcom.gov.uk.

The British Law Commission Annual Report. "The Forty-First Annual Report of the Law Commission". No pages Online: http://www.lawcom.gov.uk.

Tippet, Allan. *Introduction to Missiology.* Pasadena, CA: William Carey Library, 1987.

Terry, John Mark et al. (eds.). *Missiology: An Introduction to the Foundations, History and Strategies of World Missions.* Nashville, TE: Broadman & Holman Publishers, 1998.

UNAIDS. *Facing the Future Together: A Report of Secretary General's Task Force on Women, Girls and HIV/AIDS in Southern African.* Geneva, Switzerland: Joint United Nations Programme on HIV/AIDS, 2004.

Van Wyk, Jo-Ansie. "Political Leaders in Africa: Presidents, Patrons or Profiteers?" in *Occasional Paper Series: Volume 2, Number 1, 2007.* Durban, South Africa: Africa Centre for the Constructive Resolution of Disputes (ACCORD), 2007.

Waite, Linda J. and Maggie Gallagher. *The Case of Marriage: Why Married People are Happier, Healthier and Better off Financially*. New York: Doubleday, 2000.

Waruta, Douglas W and Hannah W. Kinoti. *Pastoral Care in Africa Christianity: Challenging Essays in Pastoral Theology*. Nairobi, Kenya: Action Publishers, 2000.

Wetzel, Dale. "Cohabitation- Trends and Patterns, Reasons for Cohabitation, Meaning of Cohabitation, Consequence of Cohabitation, Conclusion". No pages Online: http://family.jrank.org/pages/279/cohabitation.htm.

Winter, Ralph D and Steven C. Hawthorne. (ed.). *Perspectives: On the World Christian Movement*. Pasadena, CA: William Carey Library, 1999.

Women and Law in Southern Africa (WLSA). *In Search of Justice: Women and the Administration of Justice in Malawi*. Blantyre, Malawi: Dzuka Publishing Co., 2000.

Yamamori, Tetsunao. *Penetrating Missions' Final Frontier: A New Strategy for Unreached Peoples*. Downers Grove, ILL: Intervarsity Press, 1993.

Zulu, A.G. "The Vulnerability of Female-headed Households in an Urban Setting" in *Word & Content: Journal* edited by H.M. van den Bosch and C.W. Retief, 28. Lusaka, Zambia: Justo Mwale Theological College, 2007.

www.ingramcontent.com/pod-product-compliance
Lightning Source LLC
Chambersburg PA
CBHW061734270326
41928CB00011B/2225